EVOLVING
Relationships

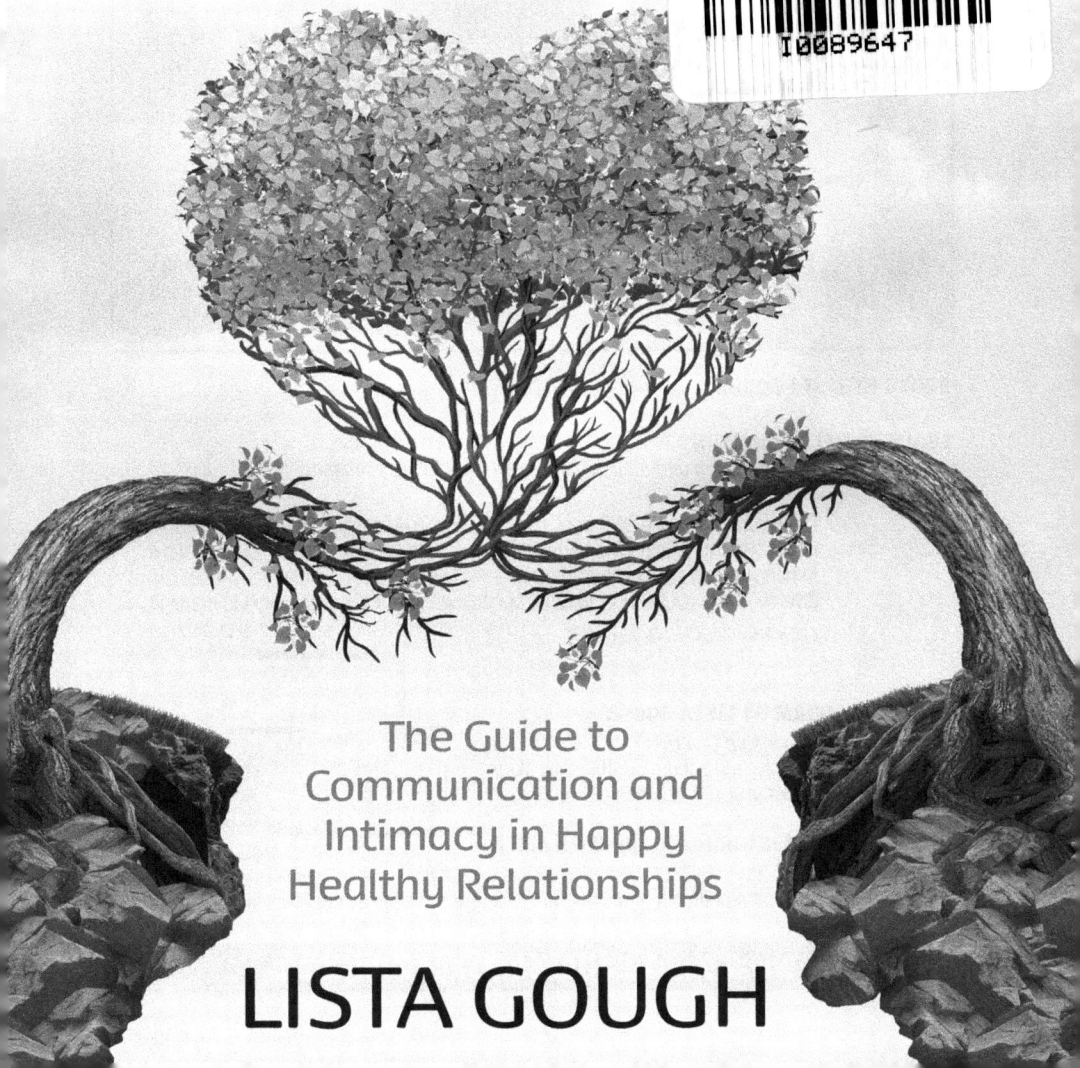

The Guide to
Communication and
Intimacy in Happy
Healthy Relationships

LISTA GOUGH

WHY NOT HAVE LISTA GOUGH AS A GUEST SPEAKER ON YOUR NEXT PODCAST, SEMINAR OR EVENT?

YOUR RELATIONSHIPS ACADEMY – LISTA GOUGH

Email: yourrelationshipsacademy@gmail.com
Phone: + 61409 670 370
Website: www.yourrelationships.com

This is a callout to Wellness Practitioners and others with an interest in better relationships, relationship diversity, and communication and intimacy in relationships! Lista Gough has answered the call and is available for speaking opportunities, private sessions and mentoring.

Lista is the founder and Principal of Your Relationships Academy. She is a dedicated Mentor to Wellness Practitioners who feel the calling to help others with relationship challenges or to specialize by training to support members of the growing diverse relationships community. With over 150 known genders and a long list of relationship preferences, understanding this community and being informed to support its members offers you the potential to expand your practice and be booked out and valued. Word spreads fast in this community, when a skilled practitioner is schooled in the terminology and unique challenges faced by its members, word of mouth will mean your business soars.

Lista is a counselor with 20 plus years working in mental health, specializing in relationships and trauma. Throughout almost 30 years of marriage (to the one person), Lista learned what it takes to make great relationships great. It isn't magically about being with THE ONE, it is about the rich tapestry of ALL our relationships, including the one with ourselves.

BOOKS BY LISTA GOUGH

EVOLVING RELATIONSHIPS
The Guide to Communication and Intimacy in Happy Healthy Relationships

Do you believe in the ONE person to fulfil your relationship needs? What happens when the ONE doesn't live up to who you thought they would be? Discover how to handle tricky relationships, baggage that holds you back, the many faces of diverse relationships, how to reset boundaries after challenges, how to manage expectations and much more.

ONLINE PROGRAM BY LISTA GOUGH
Certificate in Relationship Diversity
Enrol in Lista's Program and become Certified by **Your Relationships Academy** in Relationship Diversity.

PRACTITIONER MENTORING GROUP WITH LISTA GOUGH
Group and individual mentoring opportunities with Lista are available by application.

EVOLVING
Relationships

The Guide to
Communication and
Intimacy in Happy
Healthy Relationships

LISTA GOUGH

Brought to you by:
Mind Potential Publishing

Author: Lista Gough
Title: Evolving Relationships
ISBN Paperback: 978-1-922380-15-9
ISBN Kindle: 978-1-922380-17-3

A catalogue record for this book is available from the National Library of Australia

Category: Self Help Techniques | Interpersonal Relations

Publisher: Mind Potential Publishing
Division of Mind Design Centre Pty Ltd, PO Box 6094, Maroochydore BC Queensland, Australia, 4558. International
Phone: +61 405 138 567 Australia Phone: 1300 664 544
www.thepotentialist.com | www.yourrelationships.com

Cover design by NGirl Design | www.ngirldesign.com.au

DEDICATION

To my family: For providing me with the challenges needed to grow, for always being there and reminding me what's important. The world is a much more interesting place with you in it. You're all a bit special, falling somewhere on the spectrum, and that's what makes you beautiful. Love you infinitely.

With gratitude to Denice Harrison, my mum, who has always had faith in my writing ability and has supported me in endless ways. Much love and respect to you, Mum. You have always been someone I've looked up to and your strength never ceases to inspire me.

Appreciation for on-going support from Victoria, who prompted the initial idea of this book and who has provided me with in-depth conversations balanced with wit and humor. I value our connection beyond measure.

To Monique & Paul: for just being your awesome selves. Your presence in my life brings me joy, enthusiasm and comfort. I love the way we met; best book club ever!

CONTENTS

Introduction   1

Chapter 1:   Who's Pulling the Strings in this
                 Relationship   7

Chapter 2:   Defining Healthy Boundaries   15

Chapter 3:   Managing Expectations   23

Chapter 4:   Moving Beyond Baggage   35

Chapter 5:   Communication, Communication,
                 Communication   45

Chapter 6:   Intimacy is More than Sex   55

Chapter 7:   Respect You, Respect Me   63

Chapter 8:   Commitment to Showing Up   69

Chapter 9:   Relationship Diversity – Do it Your Way   75

Chapter 10: Who's Judging Who   91

Happy Healthy Relationships   99

Glossary of Terms   102

Appendix   107

Acknowledgements   108

References & Recommended Reading   109

Meet the Author   111

Testimonials   112

INTRODUCTION

Let's Begin

"I believe that the quality of our relationships determines the quality or our lives." Esther Perel

Relationships weave through every aspect of our lives, yet we rarely take the time to consciously focus on them. To see how they're functioning. *If* they're functioning. Our relationships with others underpin every aspect of our lives.

When our relationships are flowing well, our lives often seem to flow well too. Our relationships provide an essential pillar in our lives, our need for belonging. I think of relationships like the night-sky filled with stars (my favorite time of day). Each star is beautiful and unique. As are each of my relationships.

> "To be human is to belong. Belonging is a circle that embraces everything... The word "belonging" holds together two fundamental aspects of life: being and longing, the Longing of our being and the Being of our longing". John O'Donohue

There are so many relationships that we have; with our parents, siblings, children, nieces, nephews, aunts, uncles, grandparents, friends, room-mates, romantic, sexual, kink, and so many that cannot be defined. Why is it here in Western culture, that we tend to put so much emphasis on romantic and sexual relations above and beyond all else to the point where a lot of our other relations tend to fall away?

Loving others means understanding them in a special way, and as author of "Living Intimately", Judith Blackstone says, "The ability to love goes beyond having an emotional response to or understanding another person. It requires a capacity for contact, and this contact does not necessarily have to be physical. It can include how you speak to them, the emotions you display to them, and the awareness you have about them. It's about being in tune with another person."

It strikes me as odd when asked, "Are you in a relationship?" Of course. I have many. For me, a relationship means relating to another. In fact, you and I are now having a relationship, albeit a distant one (though how much this book resonates with you will determine the depth of your feeling toward this relationship). We have many relationships. Some will be closer than others and they will tend to fluctuate according to circumstances and feelings. What a relationship looks like is entirely up to the individuals within it.

Ultimately your relationships are about you. The type of relationship you have with someone will depend on your disposition, circumstances, communication ability, negotiation & boundaries. Every relationship is important. Every relationship is providing important pieces of information about who you are, about your world and your place in it. Your relationships are constantly changing, as you are constantly changing. Sometimes it's your relationships that help you evolve as a person, and sometimes it's you that helps evolve or collapse your relationships. If you want your relationship to change, the best way to do it is to start by changing yourself. Start by becoming more aware, more present, and learning effective strategies and techniques for communication and intimacy.

Throughout my life I've been fortunate to have many people to help support & nurture my way through the world. Born into the world prematurely, I was adopted at the age of 6 weeks. Growing up trying to find where I belonged was challenging. When I was 9 years old, I had this amazing cat. I know, it sounds a little out there, but I spent a lot of my time with him. From him I learned to be still, to be quiet enough to listen to the world around me and within me. He taught me how to center. Most of all he taught me that it didn't matter if I was alone in the world because I was here, and cats just don't seem to care about belonging to people, because they belong to the world.

I didn't get it at first. I belong because I belong to the world. I suppose having a cat as my guru during my tentative years had a hand in the way I saw the world. My perception of how things work and didn't work. I was always a keen observer. Forever watching the world around me and the most fascinating aspect to me was how people interacted.

As I got older and began to take an interest in dating, I realized I liked the idea of open relationships. Even in my teenage years. This is not to say it all went smoothly. Far from it. Jealousy & insecurities became intermittent companions sometimes for me or sometimes for my partners.

It may seem difficult to fathom but having multiple relationships has been an absolute gift. You see, it's really given me so much practice to work on myself, my perspective, my inner & outer communication and security.

The last one may have surprised you. Here's an example of what I mean: my husband of over 25 years is polyamorous. Polyamory is a relationship style that means many loves. There are several forms, which I will delve into more later in the book. Eight years ago, my husband had a break down. He's on the autistic spectrum and was diagnosed with Bipolar.

At the time he had suicidal thoughts and would sometimes try to act on them. It was a difficult time for him and for us as a family. I felt the weight of responsibility pressing down upon me. However, he would stay with his other partner on the weekend. The relief was huge. I cannot state that emphatically enough. To know that he was with someone who cared for him and would make sure he was safe was such a release for me. I also had support through my other relationships. Not to burden them down with what was going on in my life, but to give me a break, to feel joy and the lightness of being in someone else's company without responsibility or expectation.

In my practice as a therapist I've seen how relationships can make or break mental and emotional health.

This book will look at how to consciously create happy, healthy relationships through communication and intimacy regardless of relationship styles. We'll explore different relationship styles and dynamics so you can become aware of them and for you to explore your own approaches to the ways in which you relate. It's about finding what suits you best. I'm in no way alluding to one style being better than others.

I will give real life examples of how people around me have different relationship styles and how it works for them. Of course, names will be changed to protect their identities, but the stories are real. Also, if you get stuck on an unfamiliar word, be sure to look it up in the glossary.

So, let's roll up our sleeves and dig in to this delicious main course of life; our relationships. You may want to read this book from cover to cover, or you may be like me and read what takes your fancy first.

Be you and do it your way!

Lista Gough

CHAPTER 1

WHO'S PULLING THE STRINGS IN THIS RELATIONSHIP?

"Personal empowerment means deconditioning yourself from the values and the programs of the society and putting your own values and programs in place." Terence McKenna

A small child looks up at her doting parents. They seem so confident, so together, and the little girl feels secure in her world. She is bombarded with images, song lyrics, and Disney movies reinforcing the idea that love is forever and there is a Prince Charming just for her. As she continues to grow up, she encounters many relationships along the way, but none are considered as important as that quest for 'The One.' She tries relationship after relationship with the opposite sex; but not too many because then she wouldn't be a "good girl" anymore and somehow not worth as much as if she were "pure". She opts for someone close to her idea (or perhaps even her parents' idea) of suitability and compatibility.

Relationship Escalator

They date for a while and exclusivity is expected. They've stepped onto the **Relationship Escalator**. Being of the age they are, he proposes to her and she enthusiastically replies with a, "yes!" And so, the escalator takes them to the next level, marriage. Without truly knowing what's involved, what's required, or what's expected, they both jump into matrimony thinking that the divorce rate can't possibly touch them.

33% Australia	42% UK
33% Japan	51% France
38% Canada	56% Denmark
42-45% US	69% Portugal

2019 Divorce rates from statista.com

They're so in love. So compatible. Next comes a house with a mortgage, followed by kids. They continue in that pattern riding that escalator to "death do us part" unaware they've become shadows of their former selves. Their identities have become so enmeshed, they don't know where one starts and the other begins. But that's what finding 'The One' means, right?

If that's true, then why are so many people unhappy?

- Why do so many women say they don't know who they are anymore?

- Why is there such a thing as a mid-life crisis for both men and women?

- Why are the divorce statistics so high globally?

If the escalator works for you, great! You can still learn more about relationships and how to nurture those around you, become educated on what others are going through and be compassionate towards those that tread a different path. But for many of us, the escalator just doesn't work. That's okay too. There's so much out there for you to explore.

Social Conditioning

This is the process in which we are trained to behave in a manner that our peers deem appropriate. We hear a lot about it these days on social media and the topic is even popular in memes. How does social conditioning influence your relationships? As with the story above, a standard story of what we expect most little girls go through, relationships are modeled to us through our parents, community, the television shows we watch, music we listen to, and even through the education and health system.

---

relationships are modeled to us through our parents, community, the television shows we watch, music we listen to, and even through the education and health system.

Have you ever listened to the lyrics of some popular songs? Some of them are downright creepy! Take Sting's *"Every Breath You Take"* for example. *The lyrics are about obsession. Sting himself says, "I think the song is very, very sinister and ugly and people have actually misinterpreted it as being a gentle little love song, when it's quite the opposite."*

And yet many people choose it as their wedding song. Goes to show how warped some people's interpretation can be, to think that those lyrics about watching and control can equate to love.

This idea is fed to us through movies and often songs about finding someone who completes us, someone we can't live without. It's potentially a recipe for a life half lived.

A little story

I knew an older couple through my mother. They were in their 70's. They had always been wrapped up in each other to the exclusion of all else. She did have friends, but they weren't close. He passed away suddenly from heart failure. The loss was devastating for her. They didn't have children and only ever had each other. She struggled against the loss and the loneliness. Everyone around her tried to support her, but she flatly refused help.

One day she went to lawn bowls, just as she always had; she said "Good-bye" with a wave as she always did. Little did anyone know it would be the last good-bye. Unable to bear the loss anymore, life wasn't worth living for her. She took her own life that evening. This is an extreme case, but it is a genuine one.

Socially Imposed Monogamy

The other conditioning suggests that monogamy is the only acceptable way. Archaeological and anthropological evidence suggests it began in Greco-Roman times as it afforded the ability to create greater armies due to monogamous groups' ability to grow larger than **polygynous** groups. "Socially imposed monogamy … emerged in the West as a reciprocal arrangement in which elite males allowed lower-ranking males to marry, in exchange for their military service and tax contributions." Michael E. Price Ph.D. From Darwin to Eternity: *The Implications for Psychology of Evolution at Every Level (Biological, Cultural, and Cosmological). Psychology Today. September 2011.*

The modern concept of marriage

Marrying for love is an even more recent concept that has evolved over the last few hundred years.

We've been led to believe monogamy is the best way to relate. Any variance outside of it has been met with stigmatization, rejection, incarceration, and even death. There are even the subtle double standards reinforced by stereotyping. If a woman "cheats" she is considered a slut or a home wrecker; whereas for men, it is often put down to men's higher libido or a frigid wife who drove him to it. I'm not criticizing monogamy; it works for some people. It can be a beautiful relationship style when done in a healthy and respectful way.

We also seem to follow the script of duality. We follow the male female archetypes and expect that everyone should do the same because that's what's needed for procreation. However, we all know that intimacy isn't just about procreation. It's so much more. That same sex, non-binary, and transgender relationships barely get a mention (or are shunned), is a shame. I've seen so many rich and vibrant relationships that my non-heteronormative clients have given me insights in to.

Being witness to and helping clients in homo/bi/pan sexual relationships, I've come to realize the depth of commitment and courage necessary to "come out". When two partners are out of sync with how "out" they are it has an impact on the dynamics between them. How comfortable one is with their sexuality can determine how close they can become. For example, if one is struggling with their identity, they may be holding back, creating a block or a barrier between them as a couple.

Furthermore, if this person is uncomfortable, they may even hide it from their family. This can cause angst, moodiness and distrust. Constantly hiding who you are can be very painful. It's also painful for the partner who may want some acknowledgement from the family.

When we limit ourselves to the social script we've been served, we limit ourselves and our own growth.

When we limit ourselves to the social script we've been served, we limit ourselves and our own growth. Confining ourselves into smaller and smaller units we damage our community connections, our belonging, and this can impact on emotional and mental health.

Writer for Time magazine, Jamie Ducharme, wrote about 5 locations across the globe in which the local population can attribute much of their longevity and good health, to having a strong sense of community and support from that community.

What if we didn't have this social script? Or even if we did, we found ourselves on the fringe? Of course, there's always going to be a bit of push back.

A little story

There was a girl who grew up in a family that appeared normal from the outside. This little girl had a curiosity, a questioning mind but she was often told to not ask why. She kept these questions within her. In the playground when she was in Grade 2, she had two friends whom she loved, but they didn't seem to get along and would ask her to choose who she would play with. She couldn't understand this concept of choosing between friends. She felt like she was being pulled in opposite directions. She continued to grow as most girls do, with media, images & music pushed upon her.

As a teenager, she couldn't quite get the concept of exclusive dating. Really, dating only one person when you're still so young? What's with that? It isn't even dating at that age. It's more like spending time together at school and weekends if your parents allow it. Even now I see it on teenage social media and in my children's friends; the idea that you belong to someone else and they to you.

Surely a logical brain would find this quite absurd. I encourage my children to go on group dates, friend dates and take themselves on dates. Yes, the self-date is important. Knowing how to be alone without being lonely is a necessary life skill. When my kids have been in relationships, I've stressed the need (and it is a need) to remain in contact with friends, to still make time for them. How else can they evolve into well balanced adults?

Through my clinic, I've had many people come through with carry overs from a religious upbringing. I'm not here to pick on religion; far from it as I see many benefits from belonging to a congregation.

I came across a post recently by Jennifer Newman (from Make It Rain) that really said it beautifully.

> *"Here's the thing... Jesus was a disruptor. He did not keep quiet, he was not humble in the sense that he didn't keep his message to himself, nor did he question whether or not he's worthy of relaying his message. Nor did he care what others thought of him."*

I'd have to agree. What would Jesus do? I think he'd stand up for what he believed was right. It can be hard to do that. It's only through courage, self-determination and a great support network that we can ever hope to achieve this. I'm not a Christian myself, but I greatly admire the stories about his contributions to the world, his openness and ability to treat people respectfully regardless of societal expectations.

Have you thought about expanding your idea of what your relationships should look like? What if you could strengthen your connection and intimacy with others just by being open to it? I don't mean necessarily in a romantic or sexual way. You might just strengthen a really healthy platonic friendship. Having people in your life that genuinely care, that have your back, and want to spend time with you; surely this is a pursuit worthy of our time and energy.

Who's Pulling the Strings key points:

- The most common and socially accepted relationships are monogamous with the social script of the relationship escalator.

- Social conditioning herds us onto the relationship escalator

- Does this script suit you or your relationships?

·MY·
body
·MY·
~~RULES~~
BOUNDARIES

CHAPTER 2

DEFINING HEALTHY BOUNDARIES

"Healthy boundaries are not walls. They are the gates and fences that allow you to enjoy the beauty of your own garden." Lydia H. Hall

First of all, what are boundaries? Boundaries are like a line or limit that protects and respects. There can be different types of boundaries, such as: physical, emotional, digital, sexual, and time.

Boundaries are different to rules but often the two get confused. Rules are something we impose on others. The biggest distinction is that boundaries often start with "I will" and rules will start with "you…"

Sometimes our boundaries can be subtle and even we're not aware of them until someone crosses them. For example, someone may invade your personal space. They may try to talk closer to your ear or touch you in a way that you're not comfortable with.

As Terri Cole, a therapist who specializes in boundaries, points out; our physical boundaries are to do with our bodies, our sexual orientation, our personal space and "are expressed through clothing, shelter, noise tolerance, verbal instruction, and body language".

I believe the consequences of having no boundaries or, at least unhealthy boundaries will always lead to stress, resentment, possible abuse, anger and quite often time and financial burdens.

Material boundaries

Material boundaries include your finances, your material resources and your possessions. Your boundaries about these will consider who you want to share with and how. It can feel like someone has crossed this boundary when they take something from us (stealing), or if they pressure us to give them something that we don't feel comfortable sharing or giving.

Emotional boundaries

Emotional boundaries are about your personal information and what to share. For example, if you're in an open relationship, polyamorous or swinging, your nesting partner or primary partner might have a boundary in place that they don't want to know the explicit details of your time with other partners. This could also apply to children, in the situation where you have separated parents one parent may request the older child to keep their conversations to information that is related only to them and not the other parent.

Sexual boundaries

Sexual boundaries relate to your personal boundaries about your body and what you do with it, what's acceptable and what's not in the bedroom. Ongoing consent, discussions about sexual health and birth control, safe words to use to call things to a halt immediately, and open communication are all components of your sexual boundaries. An example of sexual boundaries if in a polyamorous relationship may be, *'I will have protected barrier sex at all times and have regular testing.'*

Time boundaries

Time boundaries relate to the time you share. These boundaries can be violated if someone demands too much of our time. For example; if I spend time with someone and they are on their phone a lot, I will limit the time I spend with them.

Intellectual boundaries

Intellectual boundaries include respecting other's thoughts and ideas. You can agree to disagree, in a respectful manner.
An example of boundaries I've set for my seventeen-year-old include things like:

- I would like you to be transparent about your plans and keep me updated while you are out.

How is this my boundary and how does it impact on me? Having a seventeen-year-old fail to tell you they won't be home that evening because they're sleeping at a friend's place can be worrying, uses a lot of emotional energy and wastes valuable time.

When this happened, I felt disrespected and that my time wasn't valuable. The consequence I now have in place is reduction in the phone plan limits and withdrawal of chauffeuring services for future events.

Other boundaries

Other boundaries I have may be related to my work time. I work from home and the temptation is to do housework instead of working on my business or writing. I have a couple of boundaries surrounding that. One is that when I'm about to have a Skype session with a client, I'll let everyone in the house know I will not be available between certain times and as Australian internet is rather slow, I ask that I be given the bandwidth for that time. Consequences of not respecting this boundary are that I remove internet privileges for the day.

Developing further boundaries

Developing boundaries is a skill that you can learn, and with experience and practice you will confidently be able to enforce them. Are there people in your life that currently do things that go against your personal values? Sometimes I have people who come into my life who don't seem to value my time. This is a big thing for me. People who are consistently late, constantly cancel, or who are always phone-checking when they're with me are people who I consider to not value me or my time. So, a boundary is necessary to address the behavior or limit contact with those people.

The boundary I've created is, "I will not spend time with people who don't value time" (mine and theirs). The next step is to think of ways that this boundary can be enforced. The action I'll take is to decline one on one invitations to spend time with that person. This is enforced as a boundary of self-care and self-respect. It's not a threat, as autonomy of the other person is still protected; they are still free to choose how they will behave, just as I am free to choose whether to interact with them or not.

How do your boundaries measure up?

Use the checklist in the Appendix to get a clear idea of your boundaries. Are they healthy or do you need to check in with yourself to re-evaluate?

So, remember; healthy boundaries are about protecting, respecting, autonomy and self-care; unhealthy boundaries manipulate, threaten and control others.

healthy boundaries are about protecting, respecting, autonomy and self-care; unhealthy boundaries manipulate, threaten and control others.

Healthy boundaries include things like: "I need to spend some time hanging out with my friends". If a partner responds with "if you have friends of the opposite sex, then I will be worried something might happen". This is a **red flag**. It's an example of an unhealthy boundary that attempts to manipulate you and control your behavior. It may be indicative of your partner's insecurities, which are perfectly fine; just not the way they are going about trying to address it. Further exploration on the insecurities with proper boundaries in place could lead to a much more productive outcome.

With more life experience we tend to grow more, and our boundaries shift accordingly. When we enter new relationships and interactions everything is new, and so we might take a while to become comfortable with certain things.

When we've become more familiar those boundaries may change. New relationships can test your boundaries, some you may not have been aware you had. This is a good time to discuss it, right from when you experience those feelings. Every person has the right to change their mind about what their boundaries are at any time. Keep communication open about any boundary changes to your partner and make sure you're making changes because YOU want to, not because you're being pressured, forced or manipulated into making them.

The benefit of having healthy boundaries means that your autonomy and self-agency is ensured which helps with other areas of your life.

Having healthy boundaries in place, means:
- *that you're practicing your communication skills*
- *you feel safe and secure within yourself and your relationships*
- *you're on top of your time management and your health because*
- *your stress levels are kept low and well-being is maintained.*

Remember, the consequences of having no boundaries or unhealthy ones leads to stress, resentment, possible abuse, anger and quite often time and financial burdens.

Healthy Boundaries key points:

- Understand the difference between boundaries and rules

- Know your boundaries: physical, sexual, material, intellectual, emotional, and time

- Use the checklist in the Appendix to get clear on yours

Expectations
DEPENDABILITY
HONESTY
playfulness
Consent
Expectations
consideration
Authenticity
ACCOUNTABILITY
integrity
Empathy
Respect
accountability
TRANSPARENCY
AUTHENTICITY
RESPECT
autonomy
AUTONOMY
EMPATHY
INTEGRITY
CONSENT
dependability
Transparency
EXPECTATIONS

CHAPTER 3

MANAGING EXPECTATIONS

"Often the most precious gifts of life come in ways, we neither plan nor expect." Radhanath Swami

Sometimes the word "expectations" is bandied around like it's a bad word or something to be avoided. But what if we think of it differently? Instead of thinking of expectations as assumptions, what if we think of them as possibilities? When possibilities are explored together shared goals and dreams can contribute to a truly amazing relationship.

When we think of our expectations, our needs and desires are woven through them, along with social conditioning. When you think about your expectations in your relationships (be they platonic, romantic, familial, etc.), are they respectful of autonomy, care and consideration?

Are you seeing and accepting the real person without projecting a romanticized idea onto them or the relationship? Expect to make mistakes, but also expect to learn from them. If you can accept that mistakes will be made, but that you can work through them and learn from them you know you can create a strong foundation for your relationship to flourish.

What if your expectations don't line up with your partner's? Sometimes, even those within communities where we think we've got all the answers, unmet expectations can slip through. In the initial stage when you're just meeting someone, there can be a lot going on. Attraction can blinker the red flags that alert us to a potential mismatch.

Many are so concerned with not being alone, that they try to become what they think the other person wants. Needless to say, this rarely works out. Even when you think you're practicing the same type of relationship style; you may find that it means something quite different to the other person.

A little story
For example, Harry met Jane through a mutual social club for polyamory. As you'll see in a later chapter there are different forms of polyamory.

Initially when they started dating, everything on the surface seemed to be going well. He told her that he was a busy person, so he didn't have time to date many people. Harry's ideal scenario was that he had a primary partner (that he didn't live with), and that he really only wanted one other partner. This suited Jane as she too had a lot of commitments. The fact that they lived quite close to each other added to the convenience and desirability of the relationship.

It became apparent within weeks that Harry and Jane really weren't on the same page. The expectations of the relationship were quite different. He seemed to be rushing into it as a quest to prove he was poly and she went along because of the convenience in distance.

Harry was moving into polyamory from **swinging**, trying to establish a bond through sexual intimacy; Jane was trying to establish emotional intimacy as the cornerstone of the relationship. While it seems on the surface to be a small discrepancy, overall it became obvious that the relationship wasn't what either of them were seeking. This is not to say it was a failure, but they both learned something valuable from the experience.

This is not to say it was a failure, but they both learned something valuable from the experience.

Finances

Something to consider and discuss early in the relationship to avoid potential conflict down the track is finances and how they will be handled. Your relationship styles and responsibilities can have an impact on how your finances are organized. Having partners, not having partners, living together, singularly, children, pets; can all have an influence on how smoothly you navigate your financial life.

According to Relationships Australia, one of the top causes of relationship breakdown is finances. With nearly one in three Australians suffering financial stress, it really makes sense to take an honest and hard look at your current financial status. Research done by Coe Data and developed into a Financial Stress Index, found that financial worry and stress can affect anyone from any socio-economic background.

Things you may want to consider
Cohabitation usually involves sharing costs and expenses such as rent/mortgage; but not always.
No cohabitation may mean that each person is responsible for their own finances and spending, with each person allocating their spending based on personal needs, goals, and preferences.
What kind of accounts would suit your situation? Separate accounts, merged, joint or collective accounts? Collective trusts, living trusts?
Will life insurance be considered? Health insurance?
Estate Planning: this can be tricky even in (serial) monogamy with new partners.
Equal footing. Having things in writing can help all partners feel valued and ease their minds.

Medical Power of Attorney

Being polyamorous, you may have multiple budgets depending on your needs and situation. If cohabitating, then maybe only one budget is necessary

Some families (of any relationship style) may choose to use software. I know there are some polyamory families that use Quicken, just because it makes life so much easier for them.

N.B. In the US check state laws regarding common law marriage and polygamy to avoid legal ramifications.

A basic budget might include the following:

- Income

- Housing: utilities (electricity, gas, internet, Netflix, water, etc.), rent or mortgage, maintenance, insurance

- Transport: registration, servicing, fuel, public transport, parking, insurance, licensing

- Food: groceries, lunches, eating out

- Debt: credit cards, loans, student loans

- Saving: emergencies, holidays

- Personal: pets, hobbies, clothing, beauty, gym memberships, shopping (gifts), dates, etc.

- Education/Work: tuition, books, supplies, classes, childcare

- Household: toiletries, cleaning products/ items, maintenance, tools.

- Healthcare: dentists, physio, massages, health funds.

Perhaps you may add in something like Entertainment which might include movies, rental, shows, dates etc. Don't forget dating doesn't need to be expensive (and that includes friend dates, family dates and self-dates).

Refer to the intimacy chapter for ideas and inspiration. For ease you may want to share a calendar set up for bill paying or you might want to set up a direct debit to stay on top of them and make it easier for yourself. Include a buffer that's factored in, possibly under miscellaneous or savings, to account for the unexpected.

Regardless of whether you're a couple, throuple, or more; discussing your finances will help keep your relationship/s on steady ground.

Discuss your individual goals, and as a couple or more. When you've established that you want someone in your life, be sure to ask the hard questions. Even asking questions about finances, though they may be hard, can lead to greater intimacy. Find out where you're at financially. Where they're at. If you're co-habitating, find out about debts, loans, income, child support, and other financial responsibilities.

Other questions to ask are:

- Who will look after the finances?

- Will it be delegated to one person?

- Or will it be shared?

Make sure to keep your financials in one place. This helps keep stress to a minimum. Keeping it in one place so it's easily accessible and all partners can see it means that nothing is hidden and there's complete transparency. Be sure to go over and review your budget from time to time to see if it needs adjustments. Change happens (sometimes unexpectedly and quickly) and it's best to get on top of it before troubles arise.

Even if not living together and regardless of how many partners you have and the nature of those relationships; what are your current attitudes to spending and saving, and how do they differ?

Go into your relationships with eyes wide open, keeping the nasty surprises to a minimum.

Just a friendly reminder of things you may not have considered. Naturally, we want to think the best of our important people, but sometimes things can get a little out of hand. Be aware that if you enter a joint loan, you are not just responsible for half. If your partner/s defaults, you will be chased to recoup the outstanding amount. Also, if bills are in your name only, such as electricity, you are solely responsible for payment.

Let's look at how some people manage their financial expectations:

Patricia (35) and Robert (39), married one child.

Patricia and Robert are married and are monogamous. They married and bought a house together. All expenses are shared, and they have a joint account. Robert is currently the main income provider while Patricia stays home with their two-year-old. They've made some sacrifices financially in order for Patricia to stay home as this was a priority for her. They have an automatic debit system set up for bill-paying and automatic transfer for their savings account. Robert takes care of the finances.

Lisa (40), Kevin (46), married, four children

Lisa and Kevin have been married for 22 years; they have four children ranging from 15-22 years. They are both polyamorous. They have a shared account for shared expenses, with each of them also having separate accounts. They've divided their budget into shared expenses and individual expenses. They both have an income, but Kevin has the higher income and therefore contributes more to the shared account. They have paid off their home and with the kids becoming more independent they have found there's a little more breathing room for taking the time to enjoy living. Travel plans have been factored into their budget.

Jane (48)

Jane is a **Relationship Anarchist**. She lives in a shared living space with people she's not in a romantic or domestic partnership. She lives there to keep her costs down as she prefers to spend her time out and about. She values all her relationships and so her spending habits reflect this with a section devoted to dating. She also has an emergency fund that she's set up not just for herself but also for those closest to her should it be needed. This gives her a lot of financial security, and also means that she is able to take care of herself and others.

Bianca, (24)

Ethically/consensually non-monogamous; no children; two **nesting partners**; no primary partner.

Bianca lives 50/50 with her partners. Half of the time with one, half with the other. With no children or other financial commitments, she is independent with her partners also being financially independent. She says they take turns at paying when going out for meals and dates, though how much income each person has is a factor in how often each pays for the other.

Kim, (39)

Ethically/consensually non-monogamous; one child; one nesting/primary partner.

Kim lives with her primary partner and they share the household expenses such as mortgage, utilities, etc. However, as her child is her secondary partner's, childcare costs are shared between her and her secondary partner.

Kate, (33)

Polyamorous; no children; one nesting partner; no primary partner. Kate lives with one partner and has another that lives elsewhere. To her both of these relationships are important, and neither would be considered higher or more important than the other.

This has led to having separate financial budgets with each being responsible for their own. As she lives with one partner, they both 'chip in' household expenses. She reveals that she has shared accounts before in previous relationships and found that it didn't work for her.

Amanda, (50)

Ethically/consensually non-monogamous; two biological children; one nesting partner; no primary partner.

Amanda has been polyamorous since she was in her teens and considers herself to be fairly switched on when it comes to relationships and finances. She lives with a partner for the purposes of raising a family, though she has other partners too. Her strategy is to be open, honest and upfront from the start and have some good boundaries in place. Her motto has been, "if in doubt, check in!"

Adam (40), Ben (42)

Monogamous

Adam and Ben have been in a domestic relationship for eight years. With both having similar incomes they pool their resources and set aside small allowances for personal spending. They have financial goals they wish to achieve and have similar spending habits, but this hasn't always been the case.

In the first two years of the relationship they had problems with debt and frivolous spending which sparked stress and almost ended the relationship. However, when they sat down together and discussed what they both really wanted to achieve, they then had a common goal to focus on and found managing money much easier with a budget in place. Having taken steps to manage financial stress they've also found their relationship has improved by finding creative and fun ways to date and enjoy each other's company.

Relationship Values

When we consider our expectations, you might want to look at your relationship values.

How do you want to be treated by others? Respect, care, kindness, empathy and compassion are usually included in how people want to be treated. Here's a list of expectations I have in all my relationships:

- Authenticity, integrity

- Honesty (truthful and sincere), transparency (clear, lucid, straightforward).

- Consent

- Respect for autonomy as an individual

- Reciprocation: emotional support/ investment, financial

- Accountability

- Communicate freely and without fear

- Being present (what that means to me)

- Positivity, personal growth

- Playfulness

- Consideration: empathy, compassion, thoughtfulness

- Dependability

Compromise versus sacrifice

It's not about finding a compromise, it's about what you want and need while sharing empathy and compassion. Sometimes it's more about being heard. For example:

Kathy's story

Kathy was excited about moving into a new house. She loved the spacious open plan living that would suit her family's lifestyle. However, while she was packing, she began to feel nostalgic and regretful. She loved the house she was in, it had so many cherished memories held within the walls. What she needed from her partner wasn't a solution to a problem. What she needed was support and to be heard.

They decided that after they were finished packing, they'd toast the house and share some happy memories with it. This idea helped Kathy feel better about letting go and moving on. She really didn't want to stay where she was, she did want to move on, but sometimes letting go can be hard.

This little ritual gave her the strength and support to let go in a way that suited her but also demonstrated her partner heard and met her needs in a way that suited them both. Compromises mean making choices. Kathy chose to move on rather than being conflicted and remaining in the old house and allowed herself new opportunities that come with moving to the new house.

Sometimes we make compromises with partners too. We need to hear and be heard so successful negotiation can be made. For example, if one partner is more extroverted and likes to socialize but the other doesn't, negotiations need to be made so both can have their needs met. They may choose to snuggle & Netflix at home one night a week to suit the introverted partner and have one social night a week to suit the extroverted partner (which may mean going out with others or include the introverted partner). Instead of being caught up in what we want, when we listen to the needs of others, we may find that there are still ways to get what we need. It may just take some creativity and a willingness to be open.

Managing expectations key points:

- Seeing expectations as possibilities

- Expressing our expectations and how they align with other relationships

- Habitation and financial expectations, real expectations for the real world

- Our expectations reflect our relationship values

CHAPTER 4

MOVING BEYOND BAGGAGE

"It's remarkable how similar the pattern of love is to the pattern of insanity"
Merovingian (The Matrix Revolutions)

What is relationship baggage?

The heaviness and hurts from previous relationships can seep into our new relationships.

Carmel's story

Carmel had a childhood friend, Meg, who she was constantly bailing out of trouble. In their mid-twenties Carmel had a good job and was asked to go guarantor on a car loan for Meg. Not wanting to disappoint her friend, Carmel agreed. A year later, Meg defaulted on the car loan and Carmel was then pursued by the creditors. Meg disappeared from Carmel's life without so much as an apology. From then on Carmel became distrustful of people coming into her life and constantly kept them at a distance. The experience of the past kept her from moving forward and having a rich and vibrant life filled with people who may have genuinely wanted to connect with her.

Many people's childhoods are filled with relationship baggage that remains tightly packed. Sometimes even locked and thrown into the deepest, darkest closets of our hearts and minds. It's always there though, no matter how much you may want to deny its existence. Sometimes it's easy to see the link between past and present behaviors, such as avoidance and **stonewalling**.
If we had authoritative parents who saw their children as more of an inconvenience than the individuals that they were, those children grow into adults filled with self-doubt and low confidence.

Leanne's story

Leanne grew up in a family of four. Her parents barely seemed to tolerate one another, and she became the peacemaker. You know the peacemaker type: a people pleaser who wants the world to get along and dreads conflict. She was often the one in the middle helping to smooth things over. As an adult just finishing university she was about to move out when she became ill and developed chronic fatigue syndrome. She stayed at home for the next eight years, feeling trapped and unable to move forward.

An overly critical mother and an emotionally absent father meant that she felt unable to express her individuality. However, she knew that this baggage was what was holding her back from moving on. After she came to me, she made great progress. It was an interesting therapeutic dynamic that also stretched me as a therapist adapting to her needs as a client. She called recently to let me know how great things are for her. Living on her own, going out with a new friendship circle and a new career. Almost like a brand-new person, or more the person that was always trying to get out and live. Her parents adapted and learned to respect her boundaries. After all, their problems were not hers to deal with. It's wonderful to receive an unprompted call from a client who's excited about living their life.

Letting baggage go

It's easy to talk about letting baggage go, but how do we go about it? I'm sure you've heard a lot about forgiveness and the quote that hanging onto hurt just keeps you wounded. It's true, but it doesn't make forgiveness any easier. Realizing that it's for your benefit and that it's not condoning what happened is a first step.

Forgiveness means you've accepted that the experience happened. You may still have emotions attached to it and that's okay. Learning to go beyond being a victim to that experience, the adrenaline rush from being angry, or the lethargy of disappointment, can be daunting. If it's something you've been carrying for a long time, people often wonder who you will be without your victim identity. But letting that attachment to the victim go, can also be exciting.

Who could you be without your victim identity?

Who could you be without your victim identity? What did you learn about yourself from the experience? 'what can the 'baggage' teach you? Perhaps you learned that you are

- Resilient

- you are emotionally strong, and

- you are sensitive to the needs of others.

What qualities have you had within you this entire time that you didn't even realize?

When I was a child, I was adopted into a loving home. My mother had waited a long time for me, having experienced multiple surgeries and exploratory procedures to enable her to have another child but it wasn't meant to be. She went on the adoption waiting list.

After some years she had to have yet another procedure. In pain and still recovering, she got the phone call she'd been waiting for. To pick up her baby girl. She could have refused, as I was premature and very small, but she couldn't let go and apparently fell in love with me right from the start.

As I grew, my mother had to work, so I was left with my father as he was a shift worker. Between the ages of 6 and 11 years I bore the brunt of sexual and emotional abuse. My mother didn't know. I held the secret inside me and didn't dare to let it out. It affected me in various ways. A quiet child anyway, I became even more introverted, my voice became quieter.

From 11 onwards my father kept up the emotional abuse and taunting until at the age of 17 when I saw a way out. I applied for university away from home and left, the anger and resentment still burning within me. I was an angry teen with no outlet for that anger. Fortunately, I went to university to study psychology. I wanted to know why people did things like that to each other.

I came across a book on Zen Psychology in the University library. It was a shift in the way I saw the world. I'd tried self-help books, but at the time, they made me even angrier. However, Zen Psychology wasn't about fixing me, because actually I wasn't broken. I learned the importance of meditation. Of no longer holding onto that hot festering emotional ball of hate, resentment and anger. The heavy baggage of guilt and shame.

And the world shifted. It shifted to a point where I was able to look at my life from a distance. To be more objective about what had happened. The "why?" didn't matter anymore. I was able to see how my own father had repressed years of shame and guilt, not only from when he was abused, but to the abuse he then repeated with me. It wasn't about him. It was about me, my place in the world and what I want to do with it.

Forgiving wasn't easy.

Forgiveness wasn't easy, I wasn't condoning the behavior. But I was owning my own strength and my own voice to say, "Enough". The harder part was yet to come; forgiving myself and letting go of the guilt and shame. This involved A LOT of meditation and letting go techniques.

If you want to know more about the specific letting go techniques I use then and now,
visit www.yourrelationships.com.

Fast forward to many years ahead, I hold no anger or resentment towards my father. I watched as dementia robbed him of his physical abilities and his mental capacity. It was not with satisfaction that I witnessed his dying process, but a journey of compassion. I will never condone what he did. But I also know people are complex. I don't believe anyone is all bad, nor is anyone all good. It is my choice to live this way.

There's another type of baggage.

Addiction and Love addiction.

Someone who suffers from love addiction values the person of their obsession above themselves. They spend much of their time thinking about the other person, devising ways to please them, and ways to prevent them from leaving. They fear abandonment and instead create **enmeshment**.

Pia Mellody who wrote, *Facing love addiction:* giving yourself the power to change the way you love. 2003 . said "A person can also relate as a Love Addict in other kinds of relationships, such as with a parent, one's children, a mother-in law, a counselor, a close friend, a religious leader, a Twelve-Step sponsor, a guru, or a movie star."

A Love Addict has unrealistic expectations often romanticizing or idealizing the relationship and creating an unrealistic view of their partner/ the other person. They become so focused on their obsession or addiction, that they often forget to value themselves and neglect their own care. Although this seems more prevalent in females, it does occur in men too. Indeed, it may even go beyond the binary.

There is however, another type of love addiction.

The addiction to *falling in love or New Relationship Energy (NRE)*

NRE or new relationship energy consumes us at the beginning of a new relationship. The chemical cycle of love takes about two to three years depending on the person.

Do you know people who don't seem to make it beyond the two-year mark in their relationships? Or maybe it's you? These chemicals take us on a wild ride from the first sight attraction that seems to work its way through our bodies until our hunger becomes suppressed and our energy increases. These are sure signs we've been bitten by the love bug.

But for some of us, we become addicted to these feelings. That rush you get when you see or think about your crush. At the beginning dopamine is being released into the brain, this gives us that blissed feeling with a rush of norepinephrine, we become motivated, focused and goal orientated.

Too bad your goal is usually a somebody rather than an actual goal that helps out long term. By knowing this, you could use it to your advantage. Focus the energy using meditation and visualization to help you with your overall goals. That'd be a win-win! Except that our serotonin levels plummet, making us become obsessed with the desired person and our frontal cortex seems to become rather underactive. Come on! Wake up! There goes our judgment.

With our critical thinking impaired and all these love chemicals rushing around our bodies, we're on life's natural high.

A little story

There once was a woman who was just existing, not really living. There was a man, who had been a widower for many years. When their paths crossed, the stars came alive, twinkling all the more brightly, like bedazzling jewels chatting excitedly to one another. The world seemed so much brighter, like stepping from monochrome into Technicolor. Although they could not always be together due to work and family responsibilities, they could always feel the presence of the other.

Sometimes she'd walk along the beach thinking about him. As she did, the sand massaged her feet, and the sea would sweep in to hug and caress her ankles. Even these everyday occurrences, seemingly so mundane to an observer, caused within her waves of ecstasy. Every cell within her being was alive and vibrant, like she had just been reborn.

They would keep in touch with texts throughout the day. Her every waking moment was consumed with him. Sounds like the ultimate love story, right?

It was both dream and nightmare.

The woman knew this wouldn't be forever, she knew it really wasn't healthy, but she was also powerless to end it. His presence was like a drug that flowed through her being, their love like liquid gold dancing through her veins. It's like they had both drunk the love potion of Tristan & Isolde and were powerless to end it.

After five years of this, an exhausting ongoing torture of ecstasy, he was transferred for work. Initially it didn't matter. They still could feel the other, but the distance gave her space. On the beach, her favorite place to be, the sparkling water beckoned her. It was a beautiful spring day; she heeded the call and dove right in. With the cool water flowing over her, she came up for air and it was as if she'd taken her first breath. Her love was like being born, but this now, was her first breath. She knew the potion had cleared.

"What would it feel like if I gave myself the love I give to others?"

Unlike Tristan and Isolde who couldn't move beyond their addiction for each other to see a new life ahead, she did. Her love story with him had come to a close, but it was only the beginning for her. From it she asked herself, "What would it feel like if I gave myself the love I give to others?"

In that moment, as she looked in the mirror, her own eyes reflected all the love she had been giving away, it all came back to her. The self-love seeped into her pores, into every dark missing piece of her, settling in until her whole body sighed, and she physically sighed too.

What a profound feeling, so much more powerful than anything she had ever felt before, she continued to look in the mirror. She had never really experienced self-loved before. Self-loathing was more what she was used to. But this. This was a life changing moment. She would never, could never, be the same again.

Loving others was something she did to make herself feel better, to distract herself from her own shortcomings and to fill the gaps and emptiness within her. But now; now she was a complete, whole being. And how do I know that this is how she felt? I know it to the depth of my bones, the essence of my being, because I am her.

Loving others was something she did to make herself feel better, to distract herself from her own shortcomings and to fill the gaps and emptiness within her.

Moving beyond baggage key points:

- Experiences from the past can prevent us from living in the now and moving forward

- Understanding that they are experiences we had and how that affects your identity

- Love addiction as baggage

Communication

CHAPTER 5

COMMUNICATE!
COMMUNICATE!
COMMUNICATE!

"The single biggest problem in communication is the illusion that it has taken place." George Bernard Shaw

---

The go to phrase in polyamorous circles is "communicate, communicate, communicate. And if that fails; communicate!"
It seems pretty straight-forward and logical, right? Yet it's a big factor in relationship breakdown sessions. The subject of communication is very often cited as a key component to the relationship breakdown.

When I talk about communication, I want to be clear. It's not just the words we speak, or the actions we make, it's also the understanding between people. Understanding is a fundamental part of communication. It also involves actually speaking up.

When I talk about communication, I want to be clear. It's not just the words we speak, or the actions we make, it's also the understanding between people.

What happens when you don't communicate?

When you don't communicate to the other person or persons what you want or how you're feeling, the result can be irritation and resentment. These emotions can build, and it can come out sideways in quite a spectacular fashion. Getting snippy, sarcastic, and downright judgmental can really bring intimacy to a halt. If you or the other person seem to be slipping into these kinds of moods, ask, "What do I really want from this relationship?" Talk to your partner, neither of you are mind-readers.

"What do I really want from this relationship?"

Sure, you can look at non-verbal cues, but really, it's much more beneficial to speak up, be clear and get an understanding of what's going on for all parties. It's important to talk about our troubles, but also remember to talk about the great things about your relationship, your partner and the things they do.

When you're feeling unheard and hurt, how do you tell the other person?

Consider these two statements, which one is likely to have a more helpful outcome?

1. "You always leave dishes in the sink for me to do! You're so lazy!"
2. "When dishes are left in the sink, I feel like it's my job to do them & I feel upset and resentful. Can we talk about coming to some kind of agreement about the dishes?"

Rather than the first statement coming from a place of resentment and accusation, by reframing the second statement, we can tweak our intent and make all the difference to your relationship and how you feel about living in it.

When we take ownership of our own feelings rather than making it about what we perceive the other person is or isn't doing to us, we can break down the communication barrier and find some common ground to work from. It often takes practice to ask for what you want.

The language of love

With communication we can also incorporate the Five Love Languages as developed by Garry Chapman.

These five ways of communicating our love and care for others, or more to the point, understanding yours and your partner's or family's love language can help to bridge the communication gap. According to Garry Chapmen, **the** Five Love Languages are:

- Words of Affirmation, telling someone what you appreciate or love about them.

- Acts of Service, doing things for the other person such as cooking dinner, doing the laundry.

- Receiving Gifts, small gestures of love such as flowers, a card, a painting your child did, even a rock.

- Quality Time, spending time with your special people, having coffee catch ups, snuggling on the lounge.

- Physical Touch, appropriate touch with consent, a hand on an arm, hand holding, hugs, kisses.

These love languages can apply across all your relationships. Knowing yours and the other persons language of love, can help facilitate a better understanding of each other and bring deeper connection into the relationship.

You'll find a handy link to Garry's page to find your Love Language in the Recommended Reading Section.

Open communication

- Open communication allows for growth, understanding, engagement and discussion. It means that everyone concerned is able to express themselves. Using how, what, when and why can help to illicit open conversations between parties.

- Closed communication styles only allow for brief answers (like yes or no), that generally aren't expanded upon. This style of questioning is often more of a lecture, an interrogation, or when information from one side only is given.

Sometimes parents can find themselves using this method when they lecture their children about something they've done. However, opening up the communication would allow the child to find answers themselves and learn to view different perspectives.

Communication isn't something you can do on your own. For it to be effective, you need to be heard, as does the other person. Asking for what you want or conveying your meaning so you can feel heard is what we all want.

Ways for you to hear and be heard:

- ✓ Active listening by focusing on the speaker and not being distracted.

- ✓ Being clear and audible. Being a soft speaker myself, I'm mindful that I need to speak up in certain situations and with people with hearing difficulties.

- ✓ Empathy: let the speaker know you understand and acknowledge their feelings.

✓ Respect: allowing the other person to speak uninterrupted, staying on topic.

✓ If you have an important issue, bring it up face to face if you can.

✓ Texts & emails.

✓ Challenging your partner/friend to grow intellectually, emotionally & spiritually in a respectful and encouraging way; and they should be doing the same.

✓ Pick your timing. Don't bring up something that requires deep thought and discussion when at a movie theatre with the movie about to start! Find the right time to talk about things.

✓ Discussing the things that you're passionate about can help you discover things you didn't know you had in common with others.

✓ Writing letters (especially important for long distance relationships (LDR).

✓ Phone calls.

✓ Skype/video chat.

✓ Send a text message that lets someone know you're thinking about them. I love these!

✓ Say what you mean- let the other/s experience the real you.

✓ Let your guard down/be vulnerable- explore and share emotions.

✓ Talk about and respect each other's boundaries.

✓ Talk in the dark.

✓ Telling partner/friend what I love about them/ why I'm proud of them.

✓ Being present, focused on the speaker. Put the phone down, put it on silent and really engage with the other.

What to do when what's said hurts

Sometimes people say things that hurt your feelings. When this happens, give yourself time to pause. To formulate what you want to say without rushing in, without defending, or justifying. Allow the moment to pass and the emotion to move. Then speak clearly about what it is you want to say. Acknowledge what has been said. Be clear, concise, coherent and courteous, and take responsibility for what you say.

Words once said, can never really be taken back. Above all, patience. Give the other person time to have their say. Reflect back to them to be sure you understood what they were trying to convey.

Be clear about what things mean to you. For example, someone might say they value honesty and the other person agrees it is important in their relationship. But do you both mean the same thing?

Honesty or transparency

Consider this scenario. You've met someone and you both agree honesty is one of the most important things in the relationship. You just started dating so you haven't really discussed boundaries but have chatted about your previous disasters. All seems to be going well. He then goes on a date with someone else.

All is still okay. However, you learn the next day that it was more than a date. He does tell you this the next day, so in his mind he is being honest. However, it may be that you were actually seeking transparency.

So, in this instance, boundaries weren't discussed and there was a discrepancy in what honesty meant for each of the people. This is not to say anyone here was actually wrong. However, hurt could have been avoided if these things were discussed and clarified early on.

The perils of texting

In today's world I need to say something on the perils of texting versus speaking face to face or voice to voice.

A little story

Arrangements had been made for a **polycule** date which consisted of James, Anne, Kate & Margret.

James wanted to bring an extra person, Tina, who wasn't a part of the polycule at the time. James ran the idea of inviting Tina along to the group date with Anne and Kate by text. Their response was that they didn't mind someone else coming along. However, James took over a week to get around to texting Margret. Margret's response was negative. She felt this was special time for the four of them and bringing in someone that she hadn't met would change the group dynamic.

Although Anne's response was that she didn't mind, she was concerned that the delay in telling Margret and the delivery was a little off. It resulted in a breakdown of the relationship between James and Anne with James telling her he didn't see why he should have to tell others what his relationships were as he was a Relationship Anarchist.

Anne believed it wasn't a matter of what you called yourself (poly or RA), but one of courtesy.

A complicated situation which probably could have been avoided if the conversation were live and not done by text. Clarification could have been made early on from Anne that she thought it best to tell Margret early (to avoid her possibly feeling like she was left out and the last to know) and to clarify plans that involved the four of them.

General expectations and expectations of basic courtesy/date etiquette could be discussed to avoid future issues if they continue their relationship.

The perils of "we need to talk"

Avoid saying the dreaded "*we need to talk*" if possible.
How do those words make you feel? Whenever I hear them or see them in a text, I immediately revert to the little girl being sent to the principal's office. You know that feeling in the pit of your stomach like, "what have I done now?"
One of the critical factors for communication is presence.

Presence - Mandy's story

Mandy came to me on the verge of tears, booking in an emergency session. She'd met someone who she thought she had a great connection with. Things were progressing at a rapid rate (be aware, this can be a red flag).

Within three weeks he wanted to give her keys to his apartment. They'd agreed they were both polyamorous, and they both had one other partner. She was relatively new to polyamory and although he had been a swinger for some time, he was also new to polyamory.

Her biggest problem with this relationship was his inattentiveness. He would tell her how much he wanted to focus on their connection, but his actions were telling a different story. He was constantly taking texts and phone calls during their time together. The last straw came when he started texting during sex. She couldn't believe someone could be so insensitive. Unfortunately, I could. Although some clients have said when used properly, texting can spice things up in the bedroom; there have been a number of dissatisfied lovers with inconsiderate partners.

So, let this be a lesson to anyone addicted to their phone, for the sake of genuine intimate connection, wean yourself off. You will be well rewarded with more intimacy, connection, and finding the real world so much more satisfying.

Communicate, communicate, communicate key points:

- Understanding is an essential part of communicating

- Understand your love languages

- We covered ways to hear and be heard

- Being present, active listening

CHAPTER 6

INTIMACY IS
MORE THAN SEX

*"I crave you in the most innocent form. I crave to say
goodnight and give you forehead kisses and to say
that I adore you when you feel at your worst. I crave
you in the ways where I just want to be next to you
and nothing more or less." Unknown*

What do we mean when we say we want more intimacy in our lives?
It seems few know what intimacy actually is and many confuse it
with physical affection. Of course, physical affection can be part of
intimacy; but let's explore what the bigger picture of intimacy is,
then follow with some ideas to help you achieve intimacy across
your relationships. We'll also talk about consent, a very important
topic.

Asking for more intimacy

When asking for more intimacy most people want a closer, deeper
connection with others. It fosters a feeling of belonging and being
understood. So, this desire for intimacy can be applied across our
relationships, not just our romantic and sexual ones.

Why is it that we value romantic and sexual relationships almost
to the detriment of all other relationships? From an early age we
seem to be bombarded with the message that we must find a
mate and hang on to them forever.

Since living my life as I choose to, I've made many lovely platonic connections. It's refreshing to have the difficult talks out of the way from the beginning and to know exactly where you stand. I feel that I've grown even more as a person because I've been able to explore these platonic relationships. To discuss things in depth, to have fun and just enjoy each other's company without wondering if there's any undercurrents of sexual or romantic attraction. Romantic and sexual attraction is wonderful; however, we're really missing out if we think that's what makes a relationship.

We live in a touch deprived world. I'm not advocating inappropriate touching, what I am advocating is appropriate touch with consent. This requires communication. When we touch someone, the hormone oxytocin is released, which makes us feel happy and loved. Who doesn't want to feel loved?

I've listed some ways of increasing intimacy, use your discretion as to what is appropriate for the specific relationship, and always remember to obtain consent.

- Holding hands
- Kiss on the forehead
- Hugging/ cuddling
- Hand on cheek. Hold their face with your two hands or place a palm on one of their cheeks while speaking to them
- Massage
- Touching/stroking/brushing their hair
- Butterfly kisses
- Sit on their lap
- Head on lap
- Touching noses
- Laying your head on their shoulder
- Tracing designs on arms, legs, backs
- Moving your head to their chest and listening to their heartbeat

- Wandering hands (does not need to be sexual)
- Give a love pat when you walk by
- Close eyes and memorize each other's faces with your fingers
- Eye contact/gazing. This might feel a little weird or confronting at first, but it can really help with intimacy. Talk about the experience afterwards

Consequences of lack of intimacy

What are the consequences of a lack of intimacy throughout our relationships? For children, the lack of touch can be as serious as developmental delay and an ongoing feeling of disconnection. It's now been found that disconnection is a significant contributor to addiction and some mental health issues.

Disconnection from others and our community can also be a contributing factor to our increasing crime rates. Someone who is connected and secure in themselves does not feel the need to act against others.

More ways to increase intimacy

- Create a time where you can be still together
- Lay under the stars & just be (my favorite!)
- Dance together
- Take a walk or stroll
- Watch television, or go to the movies together
- Cook together, feed each other or share food
- Play and be silly together— e.g. Nerf gun war, playful wrestling, pillow fight
- Read books together
- Sky and cloud watching

- Learn their favorite food and make it
- Take photos together (Snapchat fun)
- Drawing or writing on one another
- Just sleeping together, sleepovers
- Go on long drives, or day trips together
- Experience new things together
- Play games together
- Share your favorite activities with each other
- Picnics
- Walks on the beach or in nature
- Cook a romantic dinner
- Leave love notes, or notes of appreciation
- Visit free local attractions (pretend you're a tourist in your own area)
- Attend free local events
- Create a memory box and share with your important person. Put things that are special to you in the box. (Tickets of movie dates, pressed flowers, flyers of events you attended. Include notes on when and why these are special memories for you.)
- Put your phone down! Engage and be present with the other person
- Create a shared playlist of your favorite songs together

One of my favorite memories is spending time with my grandfather when he'd look after me as a child. After dinner we'd have a bowl of ice-cream (a party in a bowl is what he'd call it) and sit out on the front patio.

We'd sit there for ages, just looking out at the night sky. No words were needed, just companionable silence. I loved it and miss that now he's long gone. But I still remember it and when I look up at a particularly clear and starry night, I still remember him and how I felt.

Snapchat can be so much fun. My youngest is 11 and doesn't really use social media; but she does like to Snapchat. Recently when we had dear friends from Japan visit, their daughter's English was still limited (as was my daughter's Japanese). Snapchat provided a great opportunity for them to have fun and bond together. It was really wonderful to see how connected and what a special time they created together.

On the topic of phones. They can be both a blessing and a curse. Please use them wisely. They can become a huge obstacle to intimacy. I had someone in my life (briefly) who would constantly be texting on his phone. Sometimes he'd even take phone calls during our outings.

While I completely understand there are times when you need your phone for emergencies, or to check in with the kids, it can be distracting, not to mention rude, to ignore the person you're with and spend your time texting. It has become a boundary for me. When I am with someone (regardless of the relationship.) I am 100% with that person. If the other person cannot give me that, then usually they are not in my life for long.

Long distance relationships can be especially tricky, with many barriers to creating the feeling of intimacy. I've had important people that have been FIFO (fly in fly out) and in many cases I wouldn't be able to see that person physically for months at a time.

We maintained intimacy with daily texts, photos and phone calls. In some ways it was because we had to make the effort to maintain intimacy that these relationships became my deepest and most treasured.

Sharing interests and having things in common with your partner or other important people gives you things to talk about, activities to do and share. Sharing common interests can help with intimacy and build better connections with those people you want in your life. You may even find you didn't have an interest in something until someone brought it to your attention.

Intimacy skills

You may be surprised to know that there are intimacy skills. Self-care and self-knowledge are needed and are the foundation for intimacy. Let's face it; if your partner or other person doesn't practice basic self-care such as hygiene, you're not going to be too inclined to want to spend time with them.

Self-knowledge is important in the sense that you know your boundaries and you know what you want from the relationship. Knowing what you want doesn't necessarily mean you're going to get it, but you can let the other know and negotiate. The negotiation process can be a way of becoming closer, as mentioned in the chapter on communication.

Knowing what you want doesn't necessarily mean you're going to get it, but you can let the other know and negotiate.

Intimacy requires a certain amount of vulnerability; the ability to be present and share yourself. Learning to receive can be difficult for some, but it helps immensely with intimacy because many partners like to give. If you can receive graciously, it pleases your partner. I'm not saying to accept things that hurt, humiliate or make you uncomfortable. If it's something from the heart of the other person, accepting can go a long way to bringing you together.

Intimacy requires a certain amount of vulnerability; the ability to be present and share yourself.

A note on consent:

Getting consent is paramount in all your relationships. Even children can learn about consent, and I highly recommend teaching it to them. Learning consent gives you autonomy and the ability to know what your boundaries are.

- Explicit consent is where specific permission to do something has been requested and given.
- Implicit consent is when consent is implied through actions and circumstances.

This is where consent gets fuzzy. It's best to ask for explicit consent. Even if you've been in a relationship for a while, check-in from time to time to make sure the consent given is still valid.

In the interests of honesty as a basis for intimacy, if you're in a sexual relationship make sure you keep on top of health checks and ask for that commitment from your partner/s (and their partners) too. These are common checks within polyamorous communities. No need to be embarrassed or shy.

A check-up every 6 months seems standard when in stable relationships, more regularly if it's more casual. Polyamorous and CNM communities in general seem to be health conscious and well educated. I see sexual health checks as a form of self-care regardless of whether in a monogamous, polyamorous or any other sexual relationship.

Intimacy is more than sex key points:

- Creating closer deeper connections across relationships

- I provided many tips for creating more intimacy, choose your favorites and put them into practice

- Intimacy skills with self-care and self-knowledge as foundations

- Consent across all relationships, with explicit consent being recommended

CHAPTER 7

RESPECTING YOU RESPECTING ME

"I have a lot of respect for genuine people. They might not be perfect, but at least they're not pretending to be." – Anthony Gucciardi

Respect is something we often take for granted, expecting that it will be given automatically. However, it's important to check-in and be clear about what respect means to each of us. When I say I expect respect in a relationship I'm referring to how I'm being treated. Am I being treated with due care, courtesy and consideration? It's a regard for my feelings, my autonomy, and my boundaries. Respect involves adhering to agreements, as well as acknowledgment and recognition for me as a person.

I firmly believe respect is something that's a part of people. If you're seeing someone new, be curious about how they treat others.

Kink

I need to lightly touch on **kink** relationships here even though they deserve a much deeper presentation than the scope of this book can offer.

There seems to be a misconception that it's okay to disrespect others in this subculture, mostly by people relatively new to the scene who think they understand and then want to jump in as a **Dom**.

There is more than meets the eye within the kink community. Generally, respect yourself first, then respect for others, and lastly respect for the other's kink is a good guideline. Respect in a dominance-submissive relationship will also include how the sub's behavior reflects on their Dominant.

> *"One of the most grave and inexplicable problems facing our community in general is the continued presence of downright rudeness. It takes many forms: gossip, arrogance, slander, ingratitude, interpersonal cruelty, rumor-mongering, the propensity to snub, judge, shun or belittle, a refined sensitivity to slight paired with strident disregard for how one's actions and words affect others.*
>
> *I find it astonishing, and terribly sad, how poorly we get along from the viewpoint of interpersonal relationships. Why a community like ours, whose members strive for a mature outlook on power, consent and tolerance, should feud with such violence and monotonous regularity is a true mystery." Chris M and Lady Medora ('Civility and Incivility in the Scene')*

Respect and trust

Respect is important as it's a necessary foundation on which trust can be built. If there's little to no respect, there's little chance of trust developing. If someone makes you feel less, or undervalued, or is condescending, it affects the connection.

Sometimes the more comfortable we are with someone the more likely some of our bad behaviors can show themselves.

Sometimes the more comfortable we are with someone the more likely some of our bad behaviors can show themselves. In a relationship that's valued and where the common goal is for connection and intimacy, I think calling someone on their bad behavior is valid. Remember your communication skills and tackle this together. There may be something underlying that's bringing out the behaviors. A relationship should be about love and expressing it in a healthy way.

> Ultimately, you can't force someone to respect you, but you can refuse to be disrespected. If you're being disrespected and no improvement seems likely, ask yourself if it's a relationship worth pursuing.

A little story

Zachary and Vanessa were married for 11 years, talking about opening their relationship for two years and "wouldn't it be great if we found someone, we both like?"

They both flirted online, but having kids made it difficult to go out and make a connection. Vanessa found it easier to meet people, but nothing ever came of those connections. They had a mutual friend, Anya, that they thought would be someone they would both like. They both found her attractive and liked that she was currently single and known to be bisexual. This is often called **unicorn hunting.**

In the lead up to asking Anya out, they had discussed between them that they would take it slow. They would often ask Anya out to the movies, festivals, coffee etc. It became apparent Anya was quite comfortable with them both. They decided to put forth the idea to Anya that they would like to date her and see where that might lead. All went well initially. Anya liked them both as people and was attracted to them both romantically but was only sexually attracted to Zachary.

Vanessa agreed that she was okay with that and the relationship continued as a romantic throuple. At least that's what Zachary and Anya thought. As time went by, Vanessa became more possessive of Zachary and demanded that Zachary could only be with Anya when she was there too. Eventually Anya gave in to pressure and entered a sexual relationship with the established couple. Anya felt uneasy with it but because she loved Zachary and she now lived with them, she continued.

At times she questioned if she was just their plaything and was never allowed time with Zachary alone. They went out on a group date to a party with the three of them drinking heavily. Zachary and Anya were publicly demonstrative of their affection and Vanessa lashed out at Anya. Emotions had boiled over. Vanessa was unable to contain her anger and jealousy to the point of physically striking both Anya and Zachary.

The next day back at their home accusations were put to Zachary and he left the home in an effort to diffuse the situation.

- This is an example where Vanessa didn't honor her own feelings of insecurity as they arose, sharing and communicating to find a suitable solution. She disrespected herself, her partners and the relationships.

- Anya also disrespected herself, ignoring her own boundaries and found herself in an abusive situation with the possibility of homelessness.

- Zachary felt that Vanessa had disrespected him, had no regard for his feelings and felt manipulated by her.

- Unfortunately, this seems to be a common mistake when couples want to open their relationships.

For it to be fair and healthy all parties must have a say, boundaries need to discussed and respected, common goals out in the open, and honesty and transparency communicated.

On a side note, Zachary came to me after this had transpired. In his own words he wanted to 'up-skill" so he would not repeat the same mistakes.

Respecting me respecting you key points:

- A regard for my feelings, my autonomy, and my boundaries.

- Respect involves adhering to agreements, as well as acknowledgment and recognition for me as a person.

- Respect is a necessary foundation for trust

- Connection and intimacy are more likely to occur if respect is present.

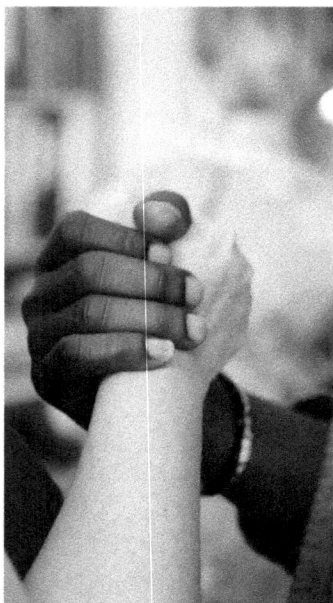

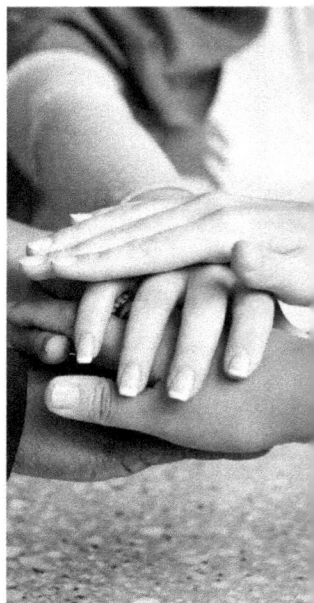

CHAPTER 8

COMMITMENT TO SHOWING UP

"Without commitment you cannot have depth in anything, whether it's a relationship, a business, or a hobby" Neil Strauss

---

What does commitment really look like? Let's break it down into the qualities that demonstrate a commitment has been made. Most people seem to agree that commitment has the following elements:

- Being present

- Honoring agreements

- Following through with plans

After over 25 years of marriage, it's not the piece of paper that keeps me in the relationship. Given the challenges we've had, it would have been far easier to walk away. But among the challenges are the gems. The moments that have provided such growth, compassion, and deep love that I would not have, had I walked away.

But among the challenges are the gems.

Commitment isn't a legal piece of paper. It's showing up, 100% being there when in that person's presence. In my relationships (romantic, platonic or familial) I am committed to being there for them, to supporting and nurturing our relationships.

Family is important to me, but I'm not infallible as a parent. I will admit my mistakes and chat to my kids about how I think I could have done better. They appreciate my honesty and my openness, and this carries in to our relationships. Knowing that I'm not some perfect person on a pedestal allows my kids to make their own mistakes, own them, and find their own solutions.

I'm committed to my mother. I do this willingly as her health declines and she continues to worry about becoming a burden. Of course, I don't see that she could ever be a burden. My commitment to her isn't just about the physical things she needs; it's the checking in, the phone calls to hear her voice, the coffee dates, the 'let's go out for Thai food for lunch' moments.

Ultimately my commitment to anyone in my life is about connection, to making magic moments together that will carry throughout the echoes of time.

Kale from Relation Anarchy YouTube channel has this to say about the key points to commitment within an anarchist's framework:

- *"They will be discussed and reached based on consent, non-coercion and mutual aid.*
- *They are an ongoing communication*
- *They help make people's desire clear*
- *They will be fluid and the terms can be renegotiated*
- *They are always voluntary. A person can choose to opt-out at any time*

No matter how committed someone may be in the moment, it's possible, if not probable, that things will change. Commitment is a living thing; it can change, it can evolve. Commitment might look the same across relationships or it may differ."

Ravyn and Eric's story

Ravyn and Eric were married young mostly because of family pressure and lack of confidence.

Ten years into the marriage Ravyn realized she was just going through the motions. She wasn't unhappy, but she wasn't happy either. She doubted whether Eric was happy and dared to put it to him.

It was an awkward conversation to begin with. However, being patient with each other and listening, clarifying and trying to understand where the other person was coming from, meant they were able to move forward with their relationship. They redefined their goals, talked about what was important to them, and sought to find a way that made their commitments to each other more personal and meaningful.

Now they celebrate the darkest time of the year, the Winter Solstice (the shortest day of the year) as a time of gratitude and what they will let go of both individually and as a couple. After a hearty winter meal, they write down on paper what it is they most want to let go of.

They speak it out loud to the other, almost like a declaration of intent, and then it is cast into a warm glowing fire. When Spring Equinox (when the days are equal and they consider what is balanced or not balanced in their lives) comes, they celebrate their ongoing commitment by having a family feast, telling each other what they love about them and how they will honor them in the coming year.

This is a deliberate act of commitment. It doesn't involve their marriage at all. No legal arrangement is needed.

Alexander and Tom's story

At the time of writing this, Alexander & Tom have been together for two years and have made the choice to move in together. Although they both remember their first date, they don't celebrate it as an anniversary. To them when I mentioned the word commitment, they both thought of the same moment.

It was after a year of dating, when they went to a wedding of a mutual friend. As excited as they were for their friend, marriage now becoming legal in Australia, they both felt a little nervous. What would the other think if they found out that I don't want that?

Each was relieved when they finally plucked up the courage to talk about it. Things had become serious; it was the depth of their conversations and the connection they felt that they wanted to acknowledge, just for the two of them. So, they decided their commitment to each other would only be witnessed by the rising sun.

They chose the morning of the New Year, renting a beautiful unit at Kingscliffe in Queensland, Australia, overlooking the water. They walked down to the beach after staying up all night from excitement. Two glasses of champagne in hand (a little bit naughty as public drinking is actually prohibited in public spaces in Australia), they exchanged promises of commitment, devotion, support and what that meant to them.

They clinked glasses to themselves, then faced the ocean, holding hands, raising their glasses to the water. What a sight that would have been to witness.

Paul and Tamika's story

Paul and Tamika have been dating for 3 years. Paul is polyamorous and Tamika is a relationship anarchist who prefers to live on her own. She's raised her child and enjoys the freedom of living solo. However, they both believe their relationship is a "serious" one with commitment from both.

Tamika says that to her, commitment is, "I'll be there for you. You can count on me". To Tamika, every time Paul turns up to attend something, he reaffirms his commitment to her. Just as when Paul became ill recently with a stomach bug, Tamika stayed to make sure he was taken care of. Although he was sick, Paul enjoyed the closeness they had, and felt secure in his presence in her life.

After he was well, Tamika went back to her place and the feeling of closeness remained. They both love their space, but also the option to stay over has its attraction as well. It is important for Tamika to maintain her independence; however, she feels every time they show up for each other it reaffirms their commitment to be there for each other in good times and bad.

For them, they don't feel a piece of legal paper says it as much as action does.

Commitment to showing up key points:

- Being present

- Making and honoring agreements

- Following through with plans

- Commitment can change, it can evolve.

- Commitment might look the same across relationships or it may differ

---

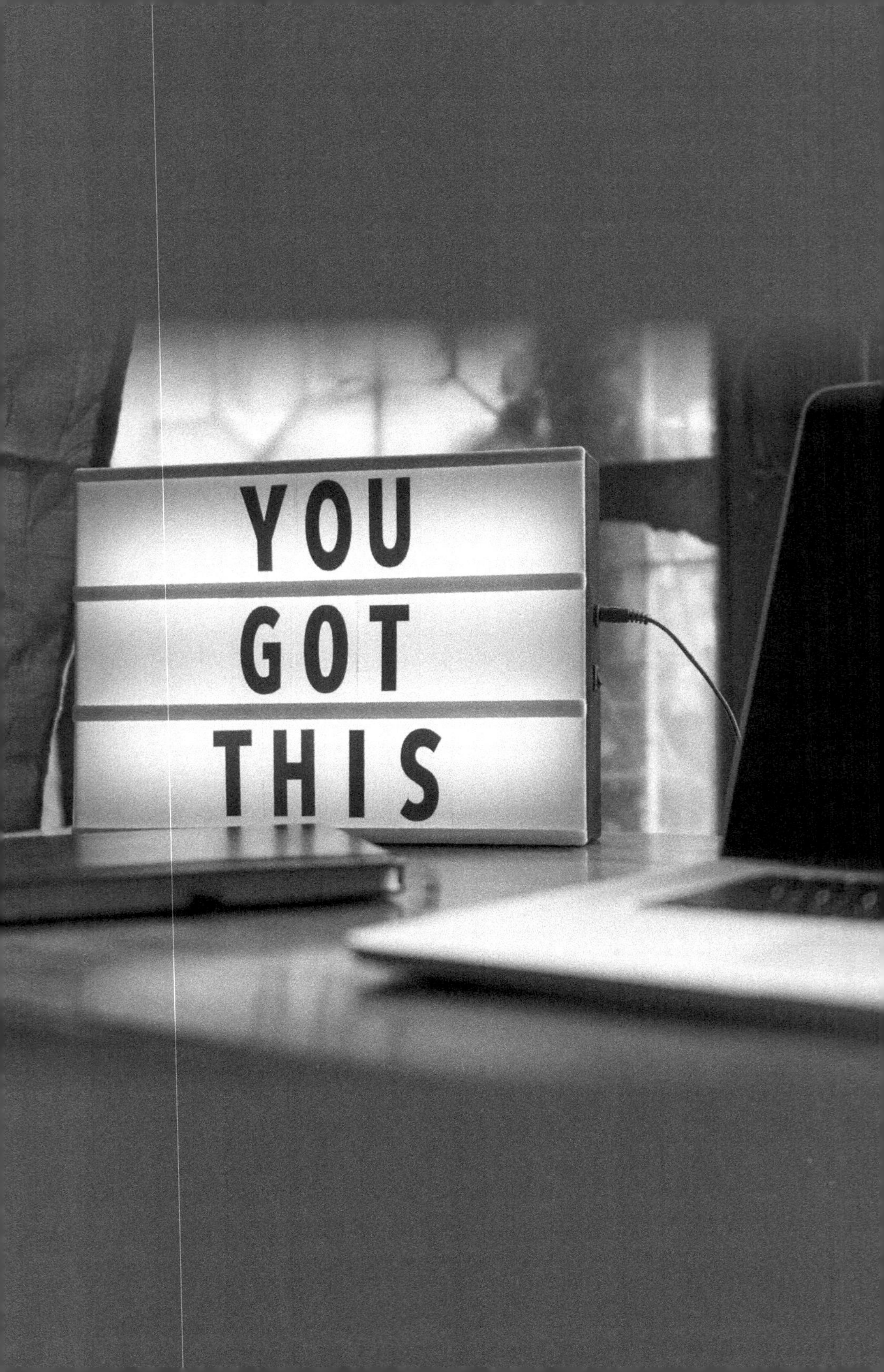
YOU
GOT
THIS

CHAPTER 9

RELATIONSHIP DIVERSITY: DO IT YOUR WAY

"It takes courage to grow up and become who you really are" E.E. Cummings

Throughout this book you will have noticed the many different types of relationships. Some are monogamous, **monogamish**, polyamorous, RA, and many other combinations that you can imagine.

In this chapter I take a look at some of the ways people do their relationships, bearing in mind I'm not saying any one way is better than another. There are benefits to staying on the monogamous, monogamish relationship escalator that we've been groomed to expect and conform to.

The greatest benefit that I can see is that it's just easier. After all, it's the way it's been modeled for us and is the expected norm. No real thought needs to go into it. It's just the way it is. There's nothing wrong with that if that's what suits you and your partner. If you're one of those people that it suits, great! But please read on, so you can understand how others do their relationships.

The more informed we all are, the less scary it is and the less misunderstandings we have.

When you step off the escalator, or perhaps you never stepped on it, the world and your experiences become limitless. To think and feel beyond what has become an accepted state, to go against all that you've previously known, can be challenging.

Friends and family will question you. You may even lose some friends over it. It happens. I've seen it many times within my practice and my community. As someone becomes more aware of their own needs, desires and wants, as they become more confident to ask for these things, inevitably there'll be some pushback.

The best way to cope with this is to become educated in the types of relationships you want, be calm when responding to questions, and realize some people are just not meant to stay in your life.

Realize that just because something is different or not the way you want to live, it doesn't mean it's wrong or unnatural.

Sometimes people will come back later when they've had time to process the information. On some occasions, clients have lost family and become estranged. Of these clients most have made peace with it in their hearts and some still grapple with it.

Certainly, I believe if a family environment is toxic, unsupportive and controlling, it's a situation best left far behind if possible. As a functioning adult, you are under no obligation to remain connected to people who do not support, nurture and help you grow as a person.

What types of relationships are there?

There are many different ways to do relationships. Here's a few that you may or may not have heard of. Realize that just because something is different or not the way you want to live, it doesn't mean it's wrong or unnatural. It's just different and diversity is not only beautiful, it's necessary.

Relationship Anarchy

"Relationship anarchy is not about never committing to anything- it's about designing your own commitments with the people around you."
Andie Nordgren

Relationship Anarchy is the design-your-own- style of relationship. Don't let the word "anarchy" scare you. Many people get turned off because they think anarchy means chaos. However, anarchy means to self-govern. Relationship Anarchy does have basic principles called the **Manifesto** which covers things such as:

- Autonomy

- Consent

- Respect

- Boundaries and

- Hetero-normativity

- It also suggests to "build for the lovely unexpected"

For me, this is the way I've come to live my life. There is no hierarchy between relationships and types of relationships. A platonic relationship can be as equally important to me as my relationship with my husband. This is not something I just woke up one day and thought, "hey, this is how my life is now". It took some evolution and soul searching and I don't believe it's for everyone.

Adrian's story

Adrian defines himself as a relationship anarchist. He likes the idea of autonomy. Although he lives in a share house and his relationships with the people in the house are important (for the sake of living harmoniously at least) he also has many important connections outside the house. They include romantic, platonic and family relations.

He has quite a close family and so he often visits them, particularly as his parent's age. He has joint care of his teenage son who he sees on a fortnightly weekend arrangement, though they keep constant contact through social media, text and video calls. They have a great relationship and enjoy gaming together as well as weekend hikes.

It was a conscious decision that Adrian made to live like this both physically and behaviorally. Ethics mean a lot to him and it's something he tries to instill in his son. Being out and about and having quite a range of contacts, Adrian enjoys friendships with people from all walks of life. He has many friends within the LGBTIQA community who frequently visit his home (Adrian is a musician).

Having this community around him, he believes is a great support and enriches his life in many ways.

Gabby's story

Gabby is in her thirties. She lives alone in her apartment in a gated community. She loves the community feel and often attends and organizes gatherings for the community and their friends. Gabby considers herself **asexual**, though she does have romantic attraction and has some people in her life that she considers to be very important to her.

Although people question her frequently about her sexuality, she is comfortable in herself and likes to educate others. While it's not something she brings up in general conversation, if there is an appropriate moment, she will let others know about it and what it means to her.

She also volunteers at LGBTIQA events and has given talks about the asexuality spectrum. She feels as though her life is full and she enjoys her work as a graphic artist, spending time with friends, and her community (both her community where she lives and the LGBTIQA community).

Gabby identifies as a relationship anarchist as all her relationships are important to her. Finding non-sexual ways to be intimate, she has had partners say they feel closer to her because there is no sexual contact. While it may seem ironic, it's allowed her to develop better relationship skills focusing on communication and tuning into her partners needs and love languages.

Polyamory

"Love shared is love multiplied" unknown

Polyamory means many loves (poly = many + amory = love).

Within polyamory there are different types. People may choose polyamory as a lifestyle choice as it aligns with their personal beliefs or it may be that it's more of an orientation. They may have tried monogamy and found that it didn't suit. No one type is better than another. Again, it's what suits the individuals within it.

Hierarchical polyamory

Hierarchical polyamory may have a primary relationship (sometimes known as anchor relationships) with all others being secondary or tertiary. This hierarchy may be determined when a formerly monogamous relationship opens into a polyamorous one.

Prescriptive and descriptive hierarchy

There may also be the difference between prescriptive and descriptive hierarchy. For example, prescriptive hierarchy is based on an agreement beforehand that this is the way the relationship and any others outside the primary will be. In contrast descriptive hierarchy might be more of a description in that someone may be a 'secondary' based only on factors such as distance and/or time, not on the level of affection, intimacy or esteem.

- For some people being a "secondary" can be negative in that they feel they are of less importance.

- For others being secondary can mean less pressure and keeps the relationship light, though still far from casual.

Ben and Linda's story

Ben and Linda have been married for 10 years. This is their primary relationship and they have joint goals. They both have secondary relationships and enjoy the company of their other partners.

They feel that having other partners helps them to appreciate each other all the more. They have limited time to spend outside their primary relationship. Linda's other partner also has limited time and enjoys their connection as being something more than casual, but less heavy than the primary one he has with his wife.

Ben's other partner, however, has had some challenges with the secondary label and has been disappointed with the **veto** privileges that Linda has. For her having someone else outside of her relationship having so much power challenges her desire for a deeper connection with Ben.

Non-hierarchical or egalitarian polyamory

As its name suggests, this is the idea that all romantic and sexual relationships are equal, with no secondaries or tertiaries. However, there's still a hierarchy or preference over platonic relationships. Within this structure privilege is kept to a minimum. Sometimes this style may include **Polyfidelity** which means that those individuals within these relationships are exclusive to each other.

Michelle and Rob and Christine and Jeff's story

Michelle and Rob have been polyamorous for 12 years and Christine and Jeff have been polyamorous for eight years.

The couples met through community groups and hit it off early on with Michelle dating Jeff and Rob dating Christine. It wasn't long before Michelle and Christine were dating too. The four of them got along so well they would holiday together and eventually made the choice to live under the one roof. They are in a **poly-fi** relationship that is closed. At this stage they have no plans to open it up and are happy planning a future together as a family.

Polyamorous relations may involve married or de facto couples who see other people, singles who see multiple people, or families that live together in any number of combinations.

I came across a lovely family that consisted of a woman, two men and their 3 children. The men had fathered a child each, and with the third, they didn't know who the father was, and they liked it that way. The third child truly had two fathers. Watching this family, I could see how much benefit there was to their situation. The kids had extra adult help, nurturing and guidance. I look forward to seeing how their teenage years go!

Other types of polyamory

Other variations include **Kitchen-Table Polyamory**, so called because the idea is that everyone involved, lovers and **metamours** can comfortably sit around a kitchen table to share.
In contrast **parallel polyamory** is when relationships run separately from each other.

Solo Polyamory, contrary to popular belief does not mean they're single. It means autonomy is a consideration in the way they live their lives. This may or may not mean they live alone. It is similar to relationship anarchy, though again, there is a hierarchy or preference of lovers over other relationships.

The polyamorous community is continuing to increase. Most polyamorists follow the principle of **ethical non-monogamy**; following the principles of:

- Consent

- Boundaries

- Open communication and

- Honesty

Don't you get jealous?

One of the questions often asked about polyamory is "don't you get jealous?"

Most of us have grown up with the same social conditioning, so jealousy does come up. Some cope with it really well, being aware it is usually about our own insecurities and knowing to ask for extra support if needed. Some know it is a part of who they are and choose other strategies such as **DADT** (don't ask don't tell).

When feelings of jealousy arise, ask yourself, "is this feeling mine?"

You may find its social conditioning, words that you've picked up flit through the mind such as "if she/he/they really loved me, they wouldn't need anyone else". If not observed as a socially conditioned thought, this kind of thinking can lead to rumination and anxiety about relationship security.

Jealousy can escalate becoming overwhelming, uncomfortable, and distracting. For more on jealousy and how to cope with it, you can visit www.yourrelationships.com.

Compersion

A beautiful term within the polyamory community is "**compersion**". Having a date with my polycule (my husband, his partner, and my partner) my husband told me the next day he had the most wonderful warm feeling flow through him when he saw how happy I looked being with my partner (although I was actually happy that we were all together, bliss!).

This feeling is sometimes said to be the opposite of jealousy, though I don't see it as opposites. I know some people can even have a mixture of both jealousy and compersion.

Open-Relationships

Open-relationships differ from polyamory in that there may be instances of "Don't ask, don't tell" (DADT), secrecy and what they consider to be the need for discretion. While their relationship is open, as in they are free to take on new partners; it often means that those other relationships are more of a side, or casual arrangement.

Monogamish

This kind of relationship is mostly monogamous. However, they may allow one or both of the partners to "play" often within swinging communities and clubs. These are usually sexually based "outside" relationships, which stipulate no emotional entanglement. That being said, some swingers do develop friendships and have ongoing encounters.

Same-gender relationships

These relationships can bring with them their own sets of challenges. If the partners are at different stages of "coming out" or if they have differing levels of acceptance of their sexuality, it can put strain on the relationship. For instance, holidays such as Christmas where families expect everyone to come together for dinner, someone who isn't out to their family may not want to bring their partner or may ask that partner to pretend to be "just friends".

Having to pretend can be hurtful to the partner as they may feel that they're not as important as the family or that the partner is ashamed of them in some way. It's a complex issue with added pressure, bullying and harassment from public, work, education, and health sectors. For those that have found their way, have strong support from friends and or family and their community, same sex relationships are as deep, rich and vibrant as any other.

Non-Binary, Gender Fluid relationships

I'm only going to briefly touch on these as these relationships deserve a book all to themselves. However, I'd like to mention them as I think it's important in our modern day for everyone to understand even if it's not for them. Living in a cis-hetero-normative society (i.e., heterosexual and the gender assigned at birth) can be difficult for people who are non-binary or gender fluid.

Some move between male and female spectrum and others just don't identify as either. This can make romantic and or sexual relationships more challenging.

Ashley's story

Ashley is 25 and identifies as non-binary, using he/she/they pronouns.

They've had their challenges in relationships, even platonic ones. Recently having a special relationship where they feel accepted, respected and valued has been affirming for them. Prior to this relationship they felt like they were constantly explaining themselves.

Dating was difficult as the people they were dating would often want them to be a particular gender and act and dress accordingly. This is not who Ashley is and they found it soul crushing trying to conform.

Only after reading more about other people's experiences did they find comfort in knowing they're not alone. Reading the book, *All About Love* by Bell Hooks was life changing and helped them gain more confidence in themselves. Unfortunately, it will take some time for the world to adjust and open up about gender stereotypes and the spectrum of gender, but the more people talk about it and educate themselves, the sooner we can move forward.

Platonic Relationships

"Platonic love is a special emotional and spiritual relationship between two people who love and admire one another because of common interests, a spiritual connection, and similar worldviews. It does not involve any type of sexual involvement."
Diana Raab

As I've mentioned before, platonic love can have its advantages. Platonic relationships can be varied, from great friendships, to deep connections. There are also those who identify as asexual or **grey-sexual**.

For people on the asexual end of the sexuality spectrum, they don't experience sexual attraction, or limited attraction. For some they are completely sex repulsed and for others having sex is more of an activity than something they crave.

There is a lot to learn about this end of the spectrum. Asexuals and grey-sexuals can still have deep and intimate connections with relationships just as valid as those in sexual ones. They just don't value sexual closeness the way others at the other end of the spectrum would value it.

Fiona's story

Fiona at the age of 30, is comfortable with her life and her identity. She identifies as being in the grey area of the sexuality spectrum. Although she hasn't experienced sexual attraction yet she's open to the possibility it may happen one day.

She's a private person who doesn't really discuss her sexuality as she believes it's something personal and isn't really anyone else's business. She's had crushes and fallen in love, but live-in relationships haven't been of importance to her.

At 30, she feels the pressure from her family. She comes from a traditional background but she's staying true to herself, "Marrying and having kids for the sake of the family is outdated and everyone ends up miserable, including the kids. I don't want that".

Jaxon's story

Jaxon is 24 and has had a hard time with their sexual identity. Being non-binary, they also identify as asexual. For them they are sex-repulsed and are not interested in any kind of sexual intimacy. They stress that they have not had any sexual related trauma and do this because this seems to be a common misconception.

They're doing gender studies at university and recently became a more active member within their local LGBTIQA community. Jaxon has been in a relationship for the past year and says that the relationship seems to be going well. It's a relationship based on communication, trust and non-sexual intimacy.

Tammy's story

Tammy is 28 and considers herself to be grey sexual. She brings up an interesting point about still having a normal libido, but not actually wanting to have sex with the people she's attracted to. She says that she still fantasizes and even self-pleasures, but it's more for stress relief and that she has no desire to do those things with anyone.

She brings up the term **autochorrissexual**, the disconnection she feels between herself and those she's attracted to. Presently she's in a polyamorous relationship. She feels this works well for her and her partner in terms of having needs met.

Ryan and Lexy's story

Ryan and Lexy have known each other for five years. They met each other through a language group on Meet-up. They got along from the start. Ryan is a Relationship Anarchist and used the Relationship Smorgasbord early on in their relationship. They had already discussed common interests and values, going through the smorgasbord helped clarify where they both were with the relationship.

Lexy says it was a relief to find that neither of them felt romantically or sexually attracted to the other. Having got that out of the way they focused on their common interests. Both of them have other relationships, but value this one as equally important as the others.

Transgender relationships

From what I've seen, read, and heard, transgender isn't a choice. They are simply being who they are and believe everyone has a right to be who they are. The world needs it. Being transgender is hard not to mention dangerous and finding relationships with people who will accept you as you are without **fetishizing** you can be arduous.

Bree's story

Bree now 36, started her transition three years ago. She met Jessica two years ago. It's been hard going for them both to navigate the transition, with the stares from the public and the snickers that seem to follow them everywhere.

Bree has learned to deal with it but feels for her partner, and what she is going through too. This can make Bree feel anxious that Jessica may leave her because it's so challenging. These pressures from the outside add to the everyday relationship problems that people have. Bree has faced isolation from her family not understanding why she's "doing this", loss of access to her child, and discrimination in the workplace. But this is who she is, and if ever there was a time for her to be herself, it's now.

I include Bree's story to help everyday people understand that there's so much more going on than what we see on the surface. If someone is transsexual, it is their journey and you are just a spectator. You can choose to cheer them on and add value to their self-esteem and the world, or you can just be quiet and let them live their lives. They're not asking you to be transgender, they just want to be as comfortable in the world as those that consider themselves "normal".

> *"You know, gay, lesbian, bisexual, transgender-people are people" – Judith Light*

How can I "do it my way"?

If you always do what you've always done; you'll get what you've always got. The only way you can change anything in your life is if you change it.

It can be difficult broaching a sensitive topic such as how we want our relationships to look and feel like. However, think of the gains to be made. More understanding between you and your important people, potentially more of what you want, understanding more about what others in your life want.

Relationship Smorgasbord

A good tool to use is the Relationship Smorgasbord. It was developed by Lyrica Lawrence and Heather Orr. It's a chart that you can go through together. I've found through personal use it's best to go through it first individually then come together to discuss it.

The idea is that each relationship is unique much like a smorgasbord. With all the dishes on the table, you take what you want in the quantities you want and make up your own relationship "plate". It involves negotiation, but also an outline of what you may want to include in this particular interaction.

Surely more love, kindness and consideration in the world can only be a good thing.

To find out more here is the revised version by Maxx Hill & Phoenyx https://www.phoenyxenterprising.com/relating.html

This is your relationship. Yours and the person or persons you share it with. It can be as unique as the combination of the two of you, or you can choose to follow more traditional or non-traditional models.

We do still have social pressures to conform, but we also have more freedoms today. I would encourage you to find what suits you, and your loved ones. The world is constantly changing, so too our relationships. Surely more love, kindness and consideration in the world can only be a good thing.

"Be the change you want to see in the world". That starts with you and your relationships.

Relationship diversity key points:

- Different types of relationships suit different people and different circumstances

- Exploring some types of relationships: polyamory, relationship anarchy, platonic, open, same gender, non-gender, trans

- The relationship smorgasbord: taking what suits you and that particular relationship. It can be applied to most relationships.

CHAPTER 10

WHO'S JUDGING WHO?

"Be You. The World Will Adjust"

Judgment, from others and our own personal judgments have an impact on the world. We're not always aware that we're judging, but we can often feel the impact of it from others. This fear of judgment often holds us back from living authentically. If we're not living authentically, are we even living?

I had a client come to me who seemed too timid to talk openly about anything outside of what was considered "normal". It became quite frustrating because as her therapist, I needed to make a connection, and I felt we just weren't making any progress. As a Solution-Orientated therapist, this client was my worst nightmare. It turned out she'd been to therapy before. However, when she disclosed to her therapist, she was polyamorous, her therapist seemed to close down on the lifestyle immediately and said to her, "isn't your life complicated enough?"

Consequently, she hadn't been able to get the help she needed. Other clients have expressed their frustration with having to educate therapists on what their relationship styles are about. This wastes valuable therapy time, with the client feeling that the therapist probably got more out of it than they did.

When criticized by family and friends, try to reframe what's happened or been said as coming from a space of caring.

It may be that you're pushing a few of their buttons, coming up against the social conditioning that they're unaware of. Be prepared and do your research. Being confident in your knowledge about how you choose your life and have some examples of people who are already living that way successfully.

Usually your family and friends care for you, by addressing their concerns calmly you diffuse the situation. They may never like the decisions you make, however seeing you contentedly living your life they will learn to accept.

Sometimes, even with the best information we have, there may be family members and friends who will never accept our lifestyles. You may call a truce of agreeing to disagree or it may involve not having them in your life anymore. This is always going to be difficult. Make sure to have lots of support while you go through the grieving process.

Having support people is imperative

Your support people may be friends, partners, relatives, mentors, or helping professionals. If your support people are friends make sure they are up to the task. Just because they are your friends, it doesn't make it all right to dump your emotional baggage on them. They have their own lives and capacities to deal with **emotional labor** may be limited.

Be respectful of that. Listen to their boundaries about how much support they are able to give you.

Having mentors and helping professionals can help keep you centered, on track with your goals, and help diffuse any unhelpful thinking and behavioral patterns. Having these support people can also allow you to practice some of the skills listed in previous chapters, especially if dealing with highly emotionally charged topics.

Having support in your life and surrounding yourself with people who accept you as you are can help build your resilience. Building your resilience is something only you can do, but with help you'll find that coping with stressful situations and challenges becomes easier. Having the capacity to think things through and make realistic plans can lead to better resilience.

Having the capacity to think things through and make realistic plans can lead to better resilience.

By building on this and gaining confidence in your successes and learning from experiences that don't turn out the way you expect further enhances your resilience. Your skills in communication and managing emotions can help with handling situations that arise, especially when you remember what you want for your outcome and that you choose how you interpret and respond to people and events.

The voices in our head

- What are those voices saying?

- Is it even valid or is it just regurgitated stuff from childhood?

- Is it the voice of social conditioning?

- Are you settling for less than you deserve because you're not happy with yourself?

Sometimes people accept some awful situations because they believe they can't get anyone better and they'd prefer that to being alone.

What comes to mind is a young man who came to see me about low self-esteem issues. When he first told me about his living conditions, I wondered why he stayed. He was living with his partner who insisted he drive her everywhere she wanted to go. She didn't have a license, so she expected him to drive her wherever and whenever she wanted to go somewhere.

This seemed a little harsh, but there was more.

His partner insisted she wanted a baby. He wasn't ready to be a father due to still being of a relatively young age, only just having moved out of the family home, and the fact that he didn't have a job. He wanted financial and living security before becoming a father. This is when she applied more pressure saying that if he didn't make her pregnant, she would kick him out.

This is a good demonstration of unhealthy boundaries, abuse, and manipulation. He stayed in this situation for another 6 months. His reasoning being he couldn't go back home to his family and no one else would ever be interested in him romantically again. Fortunately, he was open to working on his boundaries, communication skills and confidence.

By applying these he was able to move from an abusive situation to now living comfortably in a share house with a partner who values him as a person. He found that his fear of how his family would see him and his own fears of being rejected for being himself, held him in this situation.

He did remove people from his life and limited contact with others. It wasn't an easy decision by any means. It took a lot of work, but he was willing to put in the effort to change his perceptions and the way he reacted to life's challenges.

Surprisingly for him, he found that those people he limited contact with began to behave differently towards him and he felt like he received more respect.

Comparing ourselves to others

It seems to be a common thing to compare ourselves to others. In some ways I think it may be our conditioning. If we're always wanting what someone else has, or does, or to be them, we're forever empty, trying to fill that void with stuff or relationships. Just as we feel superior if we're judging others and think we or our way of living is better.

I would argue though, that it is a false pedestal that easily crumbles if we were to look at the heart of it. By comparing we invite envy and jealousy into our lives. I've felt it myself, but now I ask, "Is this feeling mine?"

When I ask myself that question, I'm feeling into myself, yet also an observer, questioning. Most of the time I realize it's a conditioned thought that surfaces and I let go of it like clouds in the wind.

Judging others

We're not always aware that we're judging others. The realization can sometimes feel like a smack to the face. Even as a counselor, I've had to challenge some of my own thought processes during a session with a client.

I came in to my office one day 10 years ago to see a couple in their late sixties waiting patiently for me, holding hands. Immediately I thought, "Oh, isn't that nice. Still so in love".

I sat down and listened to their story and why they had come to see me. They were having an affair. To be honest I was taken aback at first, but it mustn't have showed as they became good clients of mine and often referred others. It was a challenging case.

They had been childhood sweethearts, but through circumstances married other people. They reconnected after his divorce and she was caring for a husband with a degenerative illness.

This case made me realize how our own judgments, even as therapists, can cloud the quality of therapy given. I feel so fortunate to have had them choose me as their counselor. It really opened my eyes as to perception, quality therapy, and being non-judgmental. I had always called myself non-judgmental before, but it really shook the core of me and what I thought it meant to be a counselor. Even though I was a relationship anarchist, I still felt the weight of responsibility as their counselor and was very careful about how to help this couple while still being mindful of her husband.

I became very much aware that I had a fear of being judged. Not by my clients, but by my supervisor and other counselors.

Who's judging who key tips:

- Fear of judgment prevents us from living authentically

- Strategies, support & building resilience

- Changing our behavior can change how others treat us

- Assumptions and the gift of opening our perception of others.

parent love respect gay child Relatives uncle Fwb business-partner kindness grandparent Friend Lover child respect relationships kindness Fwb kindness child Relative cousin lover uncle cuddle-buddy sister Fwb companion child aunt brother partner platonic kindness sister Gay love heteronormative comrade partner Fwb acquaintance Lover child heteronormative relationships love Gay companion Fwb Friend playmate respect comrade Lover cousin parent love love Friend sister uncle platonic Lover parent Friend heteronormative Lover sister uncle parent colleague aunt uncle uncle colleague aunt kindness Friend playmate brother platonic sister cuddle-buddy cuddle-buddy

HAPPY HEALTHY RELATIONSHIPS

"No relationship lasts for a lifetime. You can have the same relationship with a thousand people, or you can have a thousand different relationships with a single person. It's up to you to decide." - Annamaria Nagy

Ultimately the healthiest relationships that help us grow are the ones we can be ourselves in. This said, I believe that it is through our interaction with others that we find ourselves and what makes us content. Encountering other people with different perspectives, interests, cultures, and ways of doing things, helps us grow.

Nothing makes me happier than coming across something new that opens up new insights and interests. Being yourself in a relationship means you can approach hurdles and challenges with greater ease. Healthy relating creates space allowing each person to develop their own interests and pursuits. Having multiple connections, in whatever capacity they may be, means you're more likely to have a well-rounded view of the world and have all your needs met without demanding, pressuring or relying on one person to do this.

I've covered some topics within this book to help you on your way to happy healthy relationships. There are a few things that I really want to reiterate and stress as the most important points.

Happy healthy relationship keys

- First of all, kindness, courtesy and consideration go a long way.

- Respect is something you do. It shows in your words and your actions.

- Keep your communication open, honest and transparent so there's less room for misunderstandings.

- If there is a misunderstanding, step back. Breathe. Allow the emotions to pass and try to discuss things more objectively. We don't always agree and that's okay. Give yourselves permission to agree to disagree.

- Ask forgiveness if you do something wrong and listen to the other's perspective if you feel you've been wronged.

- No need to rush your relationships. Take your time to get to know the other person in whatever capacity you both choose. Put the effort in to get to know them while also being discerning.

- Just because someone new comes into your life, doesn't mean they have to be there permanently. As the saying goes, "You are the company you keep".

- Know that you are responsible for your own happiness. This means taking time for self-care, self-time, and self -pleasure. Do something you enjoy, that you look forward to. Taking this time helps you be more balanced but also more interesting. When you take time to do things for yourself and it's something you enjoy, it shows! This also applies to not waiting around for others. Don't wait around to be invited out by others, live!

- Just because a relationship ends doesn't mean it or you failed. It just means that your needs, wants and goals are no longer in alignment with each other. I would like to see an end to the idea that separation or divorce is a failure of some kind. It really does nothing for the people involved except to make them feel worse about a situation that no longer works. Move on people!

What is the outcome that you want?

Think about this in terms of your relationship and let that weave its way through your actions and communication. Think about the underlying needs and desires and let them be your guide when you're with the other person.

Our relationships are much like trees in a forest with our roots reaching out to make connection. The giant interconnections of fungi within the soil, the World Wide Web, are like our communication.

The quality of the fungi determines the strength of connection to others, but also carries the connections far and wide, just as the quality of our communication can strengthen our connection to each other.

Remember that as the trees release their breath, we breathe in. The breath connects us. It connects us to everything that lives, is living and will ever live. We are connected. May the forest be with you.

Lista Gough

GLOSSARY
OF TERMS

Agreement: Negotiated terms, behaviors, and communication between people in a relationship. Agreements can always be renegotiated as required.

Asexual: Someone who doesn't experience sexual attraction and is considered a sexual orientation. Unlike abstinence or celibacy, asexuality is not based on choice. **Demi-sexuality**; sexual attraction only after an emotional bond is formed, is often included in the asexual end of the sexuality spectrum. **Gray-sexuality**: also known as gray A or gray Ace; limited sexual attraction. Sexual attraction isn't binary, it's a spectrum.

Autochorrissexual: Disconnection between oneself and the object of arousal or sexual situations. For example, an autochorrissexual may watch porn, but may not wish to physically participate in it. This falls within the asexual label.

Autonomy: having self-agency, self-governed. The ability and right to determine one's own decisions and choices.

Consensual Non-Monogamy or ethical non-monogamy (CNM): An umbrella term that covers most ethical practices outside of monogamy, including but not limited to polyamory, swinging, friend with benefits, relationship anarchy and open relationships.

Compersion: The feeling of warmth and happiness that a partner is happy

DADT: Don't Ask Don't Tell. An agreement between partners that what happens outside the relationship will not be talked about within the relationship.

Dominant (Dome, Domme, Mistress): The term describes a particular dynamic and role within a kink style (D/s) relationship. From onlookers it may appear that the Dominant has all the power, however this is a dynamic of intricate power balance, as it is the submissive that allows the Dominant to have the power. Agreed upon rules at the beginning of the relationship are a must as misuse, abuse, and misunderstanding can undermine the integrity of this type of relationship. This is a very basic interpretation as the topic is very deep and complex.

Egalitarian Polyamory: relationships that are fair and equitable.

Emotional Labor: The time and effort invested in the management of feelings and emotions.

Enmeshment: describes a relationship where the people within it merge identities, and there are no clear boundaries.

Ethical Non-Monogamy: Also known as consensual non-monogamy. Relationships that involve more than two that has enthusiastic consent and respect as its core and with everyone aware of the arrangements made.

Fetishizing: Turning something or someone into a romantic or sexualized object, rather than treating them as the person they are.

Hierarchy, polyamory: Ranking in order of importance. Usually uses primary, secondary and tertiary descriptives.

Hetero-normative: the world view that denotes hetero-sexuality as the preferred and "normal" sexuality

Intimacy (healthy): Connection or closeness, this may not necessarily involve sexual contact.

Jealousy: feelings of upset or discomfort that your partner is with someone else or taking an interest in someone else.

Kitchen Table Polyamory: Describes a polycule where all members get along and communicate with each other. The idea behind it is that all members could literally sit down at a kitchen table together over a cup of coffee.

Love Addict: Obsessive love likely from attachment problems and insecurity, but also applies to those in love with love. Most likely chemically driven.

Love Languages: The five languages as detailed by Gary Chapman. The 5 Love Languages are: Words of Affirmation, Acts of Service, Receiving Gifts, Quality Time, and Physical Touch. You can find out more at https://www.5lovelanguages.com/

Manifesto, Relationship Anarchy: Regardless of your relationship style, a lot can be learned from this. Here are the basic tenants followed by the website for further clarification.

- Love is abundant, and every relationship is unique
- Love and respect instead of entitlement
- Find your core set of relationship values
- Heterosexism is rampant and out there, but don't let fear lead you
- Build for the lovely unexpected
- Fake it till you make it
- Trust is better
- Change through communication
- Customize your commitments

https://theanarchistlibrary.org/library/andie-nordgren-the-short-instructional-manifesto-for-relationship-anarchy

Metamour: Your partner's partner with whom you are not having a sexual/romantic relationship

Monogamy: The original meaning of monogamy was one partner for life. Now it tends to mean one partner at a time, leading to the term serial monogamy.

Monogamish: Mostly a monogamous relationship with the exception of sexual play.

Nesting Partner: A live-in partner. May or may not be primary.

New Relationship Energy (NRE): The rush of "love" chemicals throughout the body creating that feeling of excitement and heightened feelings. Can indicate a contrast to the feelings of an established or "older" relationship.

Non-binary: people who do not identify with the gender binary of male or female. They may fluctuate or not identify with gender at all. This may include terms such as agender, enby, gender fluid, genderless, and gender-free

Open-Relationship: A relationship in which both partners agree to sexual relations with others.

Parallel Polyamory: A dynamic where relationships do not intersect, they are kept separate from each other.

Platonic Relationship: A non-sexual relationship. The intimacy may vary from acquaintance, to friendship or more.

Polycule: network of people connected through non-monogamous relationships

Polyfidelity. Polyfi: A closed unit. The relationships between people within a unit that remains within the parameters of that unit. For example, all members of that unit or group, will agree to restrict sexual intimacy to only those within the unit.

Polygynous: A form of polygamy, with a man having multiple wives.

Red Flag: Behaviors that set off your internal warning system. Behaviors that are considered inappropriate or detrimental to the relationship or persons within it.

Relationship: A connection, bond, or way of relating to another. There are as many different types of relationships as there are people.

Relationship Anarchy: A relationship that values autonomy and boundaries where the individuals involved negotiate what type of relationship they want. All relationships are treated as unique and there is no hierarchy based on relationship status such as romantic, sexual, platonic, etc.

Relationship Escalator: One of society's social scripts for "normal" relationship progression.

Relationship Baggage: -The heaviness we bring with us from relationship to relationship
- The influence of attachment as a child plays out in our relationships
- Needs and consequences of not having them met projected onto new partners/relationships

Relationship Smorgasbord: The idea first developed by Lyrica Lawrence and Heather Orr that each relationship is unique much like a smorgasbord. With all the dishes on the table, you take what you want in the quantities you want and make up your own relationship "plate". It involves negotiation, but also an outline of what you may want to include in this particular interaction. To find out more here is the revised version by Maxx Hill & Phoenyx https://www.phoenyxenterprising.com/relating.html

Social Conditioning: a process whereby individuals within a society are trained to behave and think in a certain way, which is approved by the peer groups of that society.

Solo Polyamory: someone who practices polyamory and values their own independence.

Stonewalling: Being evasive, ignoring, withdrawal, and shut down from communicating.

Swinging: the swapping of sexual partners sometimes in group or party settings.

Throuple: A serious or committed relationship between three people.

Transgender: A person whose identity doesn't match their birth gender.

Unicorn Hunting: A heterosexual couple looking for a single bi-sexual female to invite into their already established relationship. There can be ethical problems with this.

Veto: An agreement between an established couple that allows one to call off to determine the relationship of the other.

APPENDIX: HEALTHY BOUNDARIES CHECK-LIST

How do these questions apply to your relationships? Adapt them to the relationship style you have and see how many you answer "yes" to. After you've asked yourself these questions, it could be helpful to answer them again from your partner's/other person's perspective.

- Do you enjoy being with your partner?

- Are you comfortable with your partner?

- Can you share with your partner your thoughts, worries, feelings, ideas?

- Does your partner listen to you and do you feel heard?

- Does your partner give you space to spend time with your friends and family?

- Can you tell your partner when you feel upset with something they may have said or done?

- Can you tell your partner what you like? Emotionally? Physically? Sexually?

- Can you talk to your partner about safe choices? Physically? Emotionally? Sexually (eg. Birth control, STD)

- Is your partner proud of your accomplishments and successes?

- Does your partner respect your differences?

ACKNOWLEDGMENTS

Thanks to everyone in and associated with the Mind Potential Publishing team for bringing this project to fruition. Special thanks to Maggie Wilde for re-igniting the spark of creativity that had been sleeping within me and to Trish Walker for her patience and helping me stay on task. I couldn't have done it without you.

REFERENCES &
RECOMMENDED READING

Price, Michael E. Ph.D. From Darwin to Eternity: The Implications for Psychology of Evolution at Every Level (Biological, Cultural, and Cosmological). Psychology Today. September, 2011.

Blackstone, Judith. (2002). Living Intimately. London, UK: Watkins Publishing.

Chapman, Gary. The 5 Love Languages: The Secret to Love That Lasts. Northfield Publishing. US.2016.

Covington, Stephanie. Leaving the Enchanted Forest: The Path from Relationship Addiction. San Francisco, CA: HaperSanFrancisco, 1988.

Diamond, Jed. Looking for Love in All the Wrong Places: Overcoming Romantic and Sexual Addictions. New York: Putnam Publishing Group, 1988 and 1989.

Doyle, Laura. First, kill all the marriage counselors: modern-day secrets to being desired, cherished, and adored for life. Dallas, Texas: Ben Bella Books. 2015.

Ducharme, Jamie. 5 Places Where People Live the Longest and Healthiest Lives. Time Magazine. FEBRUARY 15, 2018

Hooks, Bell. All About Love. William Morrow Books. 1999.

Mellody,Pia. Facing love addiction: giving yourself the power to change the way you love. HarperCollins Publishers, 2003

Nagy, Annamaria Lessons About Relationships From Esther Perel. https://blog.mindvalley.com

O'Donohue, J. Eternal Echoes: Exploring our hunger to belong (Bantam Press, United Kingdom, 1998), p3.

Sheff, Elisabeth. The Polyamorists Next Door: Inside Multiple-partner Relationships and Families. Rowman & Littlefield Publishers. 2013

Image Credits:

Image Belonging: freepik.com
Chapter 1 : puppet: freepik.com
Chapter 2 My Body: freepik.com
Chapter 3 Expectations Word Collage: Lista Gough
Chapter 4 Happy Girl Moving On: Renato Abati from Pexels
Chapter 5 Communication: Modified freepik.com
Chapter 6 Intimacy: Hudson Marques from Pexels
Chapter 7 Born This Way: Levi Summers from Unsplash
Chapter 8 Commitment Collage: Contributing artists from Unsplash.com & freepik.com
    Pricilla Du Preez
    Aarŏn Blanco Tejedor
    Melissa Askew
    Janko Ferlic
Chapter 9 You Got This: Prateek Katyal
Chapter 10 Judge Gavel: freepik.com
Happy Healthy Relationships Tree Word Collage: Lista Gough

MEET THE AUTHOR

Lista Gough is a clinical therapist and coach living near the beautiful beaches of Queensland, Australia. She is the founder of *Your Relationships Academy*. Her passion for human connection and relationships, impels her to do what she can to expand people's awareness of relationship diversity and the complexity of the human spirit.

Her readers, patients and workshop students find their way to her from all over the world.

Throughout almost 30 years of marriage to the one person, Lista rode the emotional rollercoaster that went with it. Throw in the challenges that come with mental illness and a large family, she learned happy, healthy relationships weren't necessarily about being with 'The One' that would magically make everything alright. What she found instead was that life was about the rich tapestry of ALL her relationships, including the one with herself, that made this process called Life an amazing and worthwhile adventure.

Lista Gough has a Psychology Degree, a Diploma of Counseling and Diploma in Clinical Hypnotherapy. She is a qualified Trauma specialist and has decades of experience as a Practicing Clinical Therapist and Counselor. Her reputation for providing unconditional compassion for the human experience means she is highly regarded both by her patients and professionals within the industry.

www.yourrelationshipsacademy.com

www.facebook.com/Lista-Gough-Author-Therapist-WorkshopRetreat-Facilitator

www.instagram.com/lista_gough_author

TESTIMONIALS

"If you want to work with someone who is an incredibly caring, generous and kind soul, then you have found such a person. Lista's unconditional acceptance of me, no matter what I thought or felt was a healing in itself. Whilst I am still a work-in-progress, as we all are, I want to say a heartfelt thank you Lista, for helping me to navigate those really difficult times. The things that I learned from and through you will continue to benefit not only myself but others too."

M. Mac, Pine Rivers

———————

"Lista, just wanted you to know that I really feel a shift in things. A few things have happened today where I have just done what was needed to be done without hesitation. Things are changing in my world! I can finally speak without feeling silly, just being me and not worrying about what the other person thinks!! :) Happy days ahead."

Kath M

———————

"Lista is insightful, knowledgeable and very present; allowing an authentic connection and the ability to feel instantly at ease in her company"

Monique Johnson, Redcliffe, Aust.

———————

"Lista has a very calm and caring 'aware' personality which flows beautifully from her personal life into her therapies. I've attended several group sessions and found her to be a wonderful facilitator."

Barbie Young, Redcliffe, October 2019

———————

"Lista has contributed many articles and poems to my magazine, 'Celestial Dust'. It is clear that Lista just loves health and self-improvement, as she has an instinctual enthusiasm to share this knowledge at the blink of an eyelash.

What I particularly adore about Lista's writing style, is how she tells a story from her personal experience, whilst on an underlying level, she facilitates teaching of her process. It is sneaky, entertaining, and most insightful!"

Sheri Elizabeth, Publisher, *Celestial Dust*. Brisbane, Qld., Australia

www.ingramcontent.com/pod-product-compliance
Lightning Source LLC
Chambersburg PA
CBHW071235020426
42333CB00015B/1486